99 Mexican Recipes for Home

By: Kelly Johnson

Table of Contents

Appetizers:

    Guacamole

    Salsa Verde

    Queso Fundido

    Nachos with Jalapeños

    Mexican Street Corn (Elote)

    Chicken Flautas

    Tamales

    Shrimp Ceviche

    Chiles Rellenos

    Beef Empanadas

    Black Bean Quesadillas

    Sopes with Chorizo

    Spicy Mango Salsa

    Tostadas with Refried Beans

    Mexican Deviled Eggs

Soups and Salads:

    Tortilla Soup

    Pozole

    Black Bean Soup

    Menudo

Ensalada de Nopales (Cactus Salad)

Esquites (Mexican Street Corn Salad)

Chicken Avocado Lime Soup

Cilantro Lime Rice Salad

Mexican Caesar Salad

Caldo de Res (Beef Vegetable Soup)

Main Dishes - Meat:

Carne Asada Tacos

Chicken Mole

Barbacoa

Carnitas

Cochinita Pibil

Birria

Tacos al Pastor

Tinga de Pollo

Chiles en Nogada

Salsa Roja Chicken Enchiladas

Beef Tamales

Mexican Picadillo

Camarones a la Diabla (Deviled Shrimp)

Chicken Tinga Tostadas

Alambre (Mexican Skewers)

Main Dishes - Vegetarian:

Vegetarian Enchiladas

Rajas con Crema

Veggie Fajitas

Spinach and Mushroom Quesadillas

Chiles Rellenos de Queso

Vegan Tacos with Chipotle Crema

Zucchini and Corn Tamales

Sweet Potato and Black Bean Burritos

Mexican Quinoa Bowl

Nopalitos and Potato Tacos

Side Dishes:

Mexican Rice

Refried Beans

Grilled Street Corn (Elote Asado)

Sautéed Calabacitas (Mexican Zucchini)

Cilantro Lime Rice

Jicama and Mango Salad

Charro Beans

Mexican Street Corn Salad

Chayote Squash Salad

Salsa Fresca

Sauces and Condiments:

Red Enchilada Sauce

Tomatillo Salsa

Chipotle Adobo Sauce

Pico de Gallo

Habanero Hot Sauce

Salsa Ranchera

Roasted Garlic Guacamole

Pickled Red Onions

Ancho Chili Paste

Mango Habanero Salsa

Breakfast and Brunch:

Chilaquiles

Huevos Rancheros

Breakfast Burritos

Machaca (Shredded Beef and Eggs)

Sopes with Eggs and Chorizo

Mexican French Toast (Capirotada)

Molletes

Nopalitos Omelette

Tamales de Dulce

Mexican Hot Chocolate

Desserts:

Tres Leches Cake

Churros with Chocolate Sauce

Arroz con Leche

Flan

Sopapillas

Mexican Wedding Cookies (Polvorones)

Coconut Tres Leches Cupcakes

Cajeta (Goat's Milk Caramel)

Pineapple Empanadas

Mexican Chocolate Mousse

Beverages:

Horchata

Agua Fresca (e.g., Jamaica, Tamarindo)

Margaritas

Michelada

Mexican Hot Chocolate

Atole

Champurrado

Mexican Coffee

Jarritos Cocktails

Appetizers:

Guacamole

Ingredients:

- 3 ripe avocados
- 1 lime, juiced
- 1 small red onion, finely diced
- 1-2 tomatoes, diced
- 1-2 cloves garlic, minced
- 1 jalapeño pepper, seeds removed and finely chopped (optional, for heat)
- 1/4 cup fresh cilantro, chopped
- Salt and pepper to taste

Instructions:

Prepare the Avocados:
- Cut the avocados in half and remove the pits.
- Scoop out the avocado flesh into a mixing bowl.

Mash the Avocados:
- Use a fork or potato masher to mash the avocado to your desired consistency. Some people like it chunky, while others prefer it smooth.

Add Lime Juice:
- Squeeze the juice of one lime over the mashed avocado. Lime not only adds flavor but also helps prevent the guacamole from browning.

Add Onion:
- Add the finely diced red onion to the bowl. Red onion adds a nice crunch and flavor to the guacamole.

Add Tomatoes:

- Gently fold in the diced tomatoes. Make sure to remove the seeds and excess liquid to prevent the guacamole from becoming too watery.

Add Garlic and Jalapeño (optional):

- Stir in the minced garlic. If you like some heat, add finely chopped jalapeño. Adjust the amount to your spice preference.

Add Cilantro:

- Fold in the chopped cilantro. Cilantro adds a fresh and vibrant flavor to the guacamole.

Season with Salt and Pepper:

- Season the guacamole with salt and pepper to taste. Start with a pinch of salt and adjust according to your preference.

Mix Well:

- Gently mix all the ingredients until well combined. Be careful not to overmix to maintain a chunky texture.

Taste and Adjust:

- Taste the guacamole and adjust the lime, salt, or other ingredients as needed.

Serve:

- Transfer the guacamole to a serving bowl. Optionally, garnish with extra cilantro or a slice of lime.

Enjoy:

- Serve the guacamole with tortilla chips, as a topping for tacos, or alongside your favorite Mexican dishes.

Enjoy your homemade guacamole! It's a perfect party appetizer or a tasty accompaniment to many meals.

Salsa Verde

Ingredients:

- 1 pound (about 6-8) tomatillos, husks removed and washed
- 2-3 serrano or jalapeño peppers, stems removed (adjust for spice preference)
- 1 small onion, peeled and quartered
- 2 cloves garlic, peeled
- 1/2 cup fresh cilantro, chopped
- 1 tablespoon lime juice
- Salt to taste

Instructions:

Roast the Tomatillos and Peppers:

- Preheat the broiler in your oven. Place the tomatillos, peppers, onion, and garlic on a baking sheet.
- Broil for 5-7 minutes, turning halfway through, until the vegetables are charred and softened. Alternatively, you can roast them on a hot skillet or comal.

Blend Ingredients:

- Allow the roasted vegetables to cool slightly. Transfer them to a blender or food processor.
- Add fresh cilantro and lime juice to the blender.

Blend Until Smooth:

- Blend the ingredients until you achieve a smooth consistency. You can leave it slightly chunky if you prefer.

Adjust Spice and Seasoning:

- Taste the salsa and adjust the spiciness by adding more peppers if desired.
- Add salt to taste and blend again to combine.

Strain (Optional):

- If you prefer a smoother texture, you can strain the salsa using a fine mesh strainer to remove any remaining seeds or pulp.

Cool and Refrigerate:

- Let the salsa cool to room temperature before transferring it to a jar or bowl.
- Refrigerate the salsa for at least an hour before serving to allow the flavors to meld.

Serve:

- Serve the Salsa Verde as a dip for tortilla chips, or use it as a topping for tacos, enchiladas, grilled meats, or any dish that could use a burst of tangy flavor.

Salsa Verde is versatile and can be customized to suit your taste. Feel free to experiment with additional ingredients like roasted garlic, cumin, or different types of chili peppers to make it your own. Enjoy!

Queso Fundido

Ingredients:

- 1 tablespoon vegetable oil
- 1/2 cup chorizo, crumbled (you can use Mexican chorizo or remove the casings from Spanish chorizo)
- 1/2 small onion, finely chopped
- 1-2 jalapeño peppers, seeded and finely chopped (adjust based on spice preference)
- 2 cups shredded melting cheese (such as Oaxaca, Chihuahua, or Monterey Jack)
- 1/2 cup crumbled queso fresco (optional, for garnish)
- 1 tablespoon fresh cilantro, chopped (for garnish, optional)
- Warm tortillas or tortilla chips (for serving)

Instructions:

Prepare Ingredients:

- Preheat your oven to a low broil.
- In a skillet, heat the vegetable oil over medium heat. Add the crumbled chorizo and cook until browned. Remove excess grease if necessary.

Cook Aromatics:

- Add the finely chopped onion and jalapeño peppers to the skillet with the cooked chorizo. Sauté until the vegetables are softened.

Melt the Cheese:

- Reduce the heat to low. Sprinkle the shredded melting cheese evenly over the chorizo and vegetables in the skillet.
- Allow the cheese to melt slowly, stirring occasionally to combine the ingredients. This should take a few minutes.

Broil (Optional):

- If you want a golden, slightly crispy top, transfer the skillet to the preheated broiler for 1-2 minutes, keeping a close eye to prevent burning.

Garnish:

- Remove the skillet from the oven. Garnish the Queso Fundido with crumbled queso fresco and chopped cilantro.

Serve:

- Serve the Queso Fundido hot, straight from the skillet. It's best enjoyed immediately with warm tortillas or tortilla chips for dipping.

Queso Fundido is a delightful and shareable appetizer, perfect for gatherings or cozy nights in. Feel free to customize it by adding ingredients like roasted poblano peppers, mushrooms, or tomatoes to suit your taste preferences. Enjoy!

Nachos with Jalapeños Recipe

Ingredients:

- Tortilla chips (enough to cover the serving platter)
- 2 cups shredded cheese (Mexican blend, cheddar, or Monterey Jack)
- 1 cup black beans, drained and rinsed
- 1 cup diced tomatoes
- 1/2 cup sliced black olives
- 1/4 cup sliced green onions
- 1/4 cup sliced pickled jalapeños (adjust to taste)
- Sour cream, for serving
- Guacamole, for serving (optional)
- Salsa, for serving (optional)

Instructions:

Preheat the Oven:

- Preheat your oven to 375°F (190°C).

Arrange Tortilla Chips:

- Spread a layer of tortilla chips evenly on a large oven-safe serving platter or baking sheet.

Add Cheese:

- Sprinkle the shredded cheese evenly over the tortilla chips, ensuring that each chip gets some cheese.

Add Toppings:

- Distribute the black beans, diced tomatoes, sliced black olives, and green onions over the cheese-covered chips.

Jalapeños:

- Scatter the sliced pickled jalapeños over the nachos. Adjust the quantity based on your spice preference.

Second Cheese Layer (Optional):

- If you like extra cheesiness, you can add another layer of shredded cheese on top of the toppings.

Bake:

- Place the platter or baking sheet in the preheated oven and bake for about 10-15 minutes or until the cheese is fully melted and bubbly.

Garnish:

- Remove from the oven and let it cool slightly. Garnish with additional sliced green onions and fresh cilantro if desired.

Serve:

- Serve the nachos with jalapeños hot and straight from the oven. Offer sour cream, guacamole, and salsa on the side for dipping.

Enjoy:

- Dig in and enjoy the deliciousness of your loaded nachos with the perfect blend of cheesy, crunchy, and spicy flavors.

Feel free to customize your nachos with additional toppings like cooked and seasoned ground beef or shredded chicken. This recipe is versatile, and you can adjust the ingredients based on your preferences. Enjoy your nachos!

Mexican Street Corn (Elote) Recipe

Ingredients:

- 4 ears of corn, husked
- 1/2 cup mayonnaise
- 1/2 cup sour cream
- 1 cup crumbled cotija cheese (substitute with feta if unavailable)
- 1 teaspoon chili powder (adjust to taste)
- 1/2 teaspoon smoked paprika
- 1 clove garlic, minced
- 1/4 cup fresh cilantro, chopped
- Lime wedges for serving
- Salt and pepper to taste

Instructions:

Grill the Corn:

- Preheat your grill to medium-high heat. Grill the corn, turning occasionally, until it's lightly charred on all sides. This usually takes about 8-10 minutes.

Prepare Toppings:

- In a bowl, mix together the mayonnaise, sour cream, half of the crumbled cotija cheese, chili powder, smoked paprika, minced garlic, and chopped cilantro. Season with salt and pepper to taste.

Coat the Corn:

- Once the corn is done grilling, use a brush or spoon to generously coat each ear of corn with the mayonnaise mixture. Ensure the corn is well-covered on all sides.

Sprinkle with Cotija Cheese:

- Sprinkle the remaining cotija cheese over the coated corn.

Serve:

- Place the Mexican Street Corn on a serving platter. Squeeze lime wedges over the top for a burst of citrus flavor.

Garnish (Optional):

- Optionally, garnish with additional chili powder, smoked paprika, or chopped cilantro for extra color and flavor.

Enjoy:

- Serve the Mexican Street Corn hot and enjoy this delicious and savory treat!

Mexican Street Corn is a popular and flavorful side dish that captures the essence of street food in Mexico. It's perfect for summer barbecues or as a unique addition to your next meal.

Chicken Flautas Recipe

Ingredients:

For the Chicken Filling:

- 2 cups shredded cooked chicken (rotisserie chicken works well)
- 1 small onion, finely chopped
- 2 cloves garlic, minced
- 1 teaspoon ground cumin
- 1 teaspoon chili powder
- 1/2 teaspoon paprika
- Salt and pepper to taste
- 1 tablespoon vegetable oil
- 1/4 cup chopped fresh cilantro

For the Flautas:

- 12 small flour tortillas
- Vegetable oil for frying

Toppings and Dips (Optional):

- Shredded lettuce
- Diced tomatoes
- Sour cream
- Guacamole
- Salsa

Instructions:

Prepare the Chicken Filling:

Sauté Aromatics:

- In a skillet, heat 1 tablespoon of vegetable oil over medium heat. Add the chopped onion and garlic, sauté until softened.

Season Chicken:

- Add the shredded chicken to the skillet, along with ground cumin, chili powder, paprika, salt, and pepper. Stir to combine and cook until the chicken is heated through and well-coated with the spices.

Add Cilantro:

- Stir in the chopped fresh cilantro and cook for an additional minute. Remove from heat and set aside.

Assemble the Chicken Flautas:

Warm Tortillas:

- Warm the flour tortillas briefly in a dry skillet or microwave to make them pliable.

Fill and Roll:

- Place a portion of the chicken filling along the center of each tortilla. Roll them tightly into cylinders and secure with toothpicks if needed.

Fry the Flautas:

- In a large skillet, heat about 1 inch of vegetable oil over medium-high heat. Carefully place the rolled flautas in the hot oil, seam-side down. Fry until golden brown and crispy, turning occasionally for even cooking. This usually takes about 3-4 minutes.

Drain Excess Oil:

- Transfer the fried flautas to a plate lined with paper towels to drain any excess oil.

Serve:

Remove Toothpicks:
- If you used toothpicks to secure the flautas, carefully remove them.

Serve with Toppings:
- Serve the Chicken Flautas hot with shredded lettuce, diced tomatoes, sour cream, guacamole, and salsa. You can customize the toppings based on your preference.

Enjoy:
- Enjoy the crispy and flavorful Chicken Flautas as a delicious appetizer or main dish.

These Chicken Flautas are perfect for gatherings, game nights, or as a family-friendly meal. Feel free to get creative with the toppings and dips to suit your taste!

Tamales Recipe

Ingredients:

For the Pork Filling:

- 2 pounds pork shoulder, cut into chunks
- 1 onion, chopped
- 3 cloves garlic, minced
- 1 teaspoon ground cumin
- 1 teaspoon chili powder
- 1 teaspoon dried oregano
- Salt and pepper to taste
- 2 cups chicken broth

For the Masa Dough:

- 3 cups masa harina (corn masa flour)
- 2 cups chicken broth
- 1 cup lard or vegetable shortening
- 1 teaspoon baking powder
- 1 teaspoon salt

For Assembly:

- Corn husks, soaked in warm water to soften

Instructions:

Prepare the Pork Filling:

Cook Pork:

- In a large pot, combine the pork chunks, chopped onion, minced garlic, ground cumin, chili powder, dried oregano, salt, and pepper.

Simmer:

- Pour in the chicken broth. Bring the mixture to a boil, then reduce the heat to low, cover, and simmer until the pork is tender and easily shredded, usually around 2 to 3 hours.

Shred Pork:

- Once the pork is cooked, shred it using two forks. Set aside.

Prepare the Masa Dough:

Combine Ingredients:

- In a large mixing bowl, combine the masa harina, chicken broth, lard or vegetable shortening, baking powder, and salt. Mix until you get a soft and pliable dough.

Assemble the Tamales:

Soak Corn Husks:

- Soak the corn husks in warm water for about 30 minutes or until they become pliable.

Spread Masa on Husks:

- Take a softened corn husk and spread a thin layer of masa dough in the center, leaving space on the edges.

Add Pork Filling:

- Spoon a portion of the shredded pork onto the masa.

Fold and Tie:

- Fold the sides of the corn husk over the filling, then fold the top and bottom to create a rectangular-shaped tamale. Tie the tamale with kitchen twine if desired.

Repeat:

- Repeat the process until all the masa and filling are used.

Steam the Tamales:

Arrange in Steamer:

- Place the tamales upright in a steamer basket, with the open end facing up.

Steam:

- Steam the tamales over simmering water for about 1 to 1.5 hours, or until the masa is cooked and easily pulls away from the husk.

Cool and Serve:

- Allow the tamales to cool for a few minutes before serving. Remove the husks before eating.

Serve with:

- Salsa, guacamole, or sour cream for dipping.

This recipe makes approximately 20 tamales. Feel free to customize the filling or masa dough with your favorite ingredients. Tamales are a labor of love, often made with family or friends during festive occasions. Enjoy!

Shrimp Ceviche Recipe

Ingredients:

- 1 pound raw shrimp, peeled, deveined, and chopped into bite-sized pieces
- 1 cup cherry tomatoes, halved
- 1 cucumber, diced
- 1/2 red onion, finely chopped
- 1 jalapeño pepper, seeds removed and finely chopped
- 1/2 cup fresh cilantro, chopped
- 3-4 limes, juiced
- 2 lemons, juiced
- Salt and pepper to taste
- 1 avocado, diced (optional)
- Tortilla chips or tostadas for serving

Instructions:

Prepare the Shrimp:

- In a bowl, combine the chopped shrimp with the juice of limes and lemons. Ensure that the shrimp is fully coated in the citrus juices. Cover the bowl and let it marinate in the refrigerator for about 30 minutes to 1 hour or until the shrimp turns opaque and "cooked" in the citrus juice.

Combine Vegetables:

- In a large mixing bowl, combine the marinated shrimp with cherry tomatoes, diced cucumber, finely chopped red onion, chopped jalapeño, and fresh cilantro.

Season:

- Season the ceviche with salt and pepper to taste. Adjust the seasoning based on your preference.

Chill:
- Cover the bowl and refrigerate the ceviche for at least 30 minutes to allow the flavors to meld and the mixture to chill.

Add Avocado (Optional):
- Just before serving, gently fold in diced avocado if using. Be careful not to mash the avocado.

Serve:
- Serve the shrimp ceviche in individual bowls or glasses. Optionally, garnish with additional cilantro or lime wedges.

Serve with:
- Accompany the shrimp ceviche with tortilla chips or tostadas for scooping.

Enjoy:
- Enjoy the fresh and vibrant flavors of shrimp ceviche as a light and refreshing appetizer or meal.

Note: If you prefer your ceviche spicier, you can leave the seeds in the jalapeño or add a bit of hot sauce.

Shrimp ceviche is not only delicious but also versatile, allowing you to customize the ingredients to suit your taste preferences. It's a perfect dish for warm weather or any occasion where you want a bright and flavorful appetizer.

Chiles Rellenos Recipe

Ingredients:

For the Stuffed Peppers:

- 4 large poblano or Anaheim peppers
- 1 cup queso fresco or Monterey Jack cheese, cut into strips
- 1 cup cooked and shredded chicken or beef (optional)
- 1/2 cup all-purpose flour (for coating the peppers)
- Salt and pepper to taste

For the Egg Batter:

- 4 large eggs, separated
- 1/2 cup all-purpose flour
- 1/2 teaspoon baking powder
- Salt

For Frying:

- Vegetable oil for frying

For the Tomato Sauce:

- 2 cups diced tomatoes (fresh or canned)
- 1/2 onion, finely chopped
- 2 cloves garlic, minced
- 1 teaspoon dried oregano
- 1 teaspoon ground cumin
- Salt and pepper to taste

- Fresh cilantro for garnish

Instructions:

Prepare the Peppers:

Roast the Peppers:

- Roast the poblano or Anaheim peppers over an open flame or under the broiler until the skin is charred and blistered. Place them in a plastic bag or covered bowl to steam for about 10 minutes. This will make it easier to peel the skin.

Peel and Remove Seeds:

- Peel the charred skin off the peppers and make a lengthwise slit to remove the seeds. Be careful not to tear the peppers.

Stuff the Peppers:

- Stuff each pepper with cheese strips and shredded chicken or beef if using. Season with salt and pepper.

Close the Peppers:

- Gently close the peppers, securing them with toothpicks if needed.

Prepare the Egg Batter:

Separate Eggs:

- In a bowl, beat the egg whites until stiff peaks form. In a separate bowl, beat the egg yolks.

Combine Batters:

- Gently fold the beaten egg yolks into the egg whites. Add flour, baking powder, and a pinch of salt. Mix until well combined.

Coat and Fry the Stuffed Peppers:

Coat Peppers in Flour:

- Roll each stuffed pepper in flour to lightly coat.

Dip in Egg Batter:

- Dip each flour-coated pepper into the egg batter, ensuring they are fully coated.

Fry the Peppers:

- In a large skillet, heat vegetable oil over medium-high heat. Fry the battered peppers until golden brown on all sides. Place on a paper towel-lined plate to absorb excess oil.

Prepare the Tomato Sauce:

Sauté Aromatics:

- In a separate saucepan, sauté chopped onion and minced garlic until softened.

Add Tomatoes and Spices:

- Add diced tomatoes, dried oregano, ground cumin, salt, and pepper. Simmer for about 15-20 minutes until the sauce thickens.

Serve:

Plate and Garnish:

- Place the Chiles Rellenos on a serving plate, spoon the tomato sauce over them, and garnish with fresh cilantro.

Serve Hot:

- Serve the Chiles Rellenos hot, and enjoy the delicious combination of crispy exterior, creamy cheese, and flavorful sauce.

Chiles Rellenos are a delightful and satisfying dish that showcases the rich flavors of Mexican cuisine. Adjust the level of spiciness by choosing peppers according to your preference.

Beef Empanadas Recipe

Ingredients:

For the Dough:

- 3 cups all-purpose flour
- 1 teaspoon salt
- 1 cup unsalted butter, cold and diced
- 1/2 cup ice water

For the Filling:

- 1 pound ground beef
- 1 onion, finely chopped
- 2 cloves garlic, minced
- 1 teaspoon ground cumin
- 1 teaspoon paprika
- 1/2 teaspoon dried oregano
- Salt and pepper to taste
- 1/4 cup tomato paste
- 1/4 cup green olives, chopped (optional)
- 2 boiled eggs, chopped (optional)
- Vegetable oil for frying

Instructions:

Prepare the Dough:

    Combine Ingredients:

- In a large bowl, mix the flour and salt. Add the diced cold butter and use your fingers or a pastry cutter to incorporate until the mixture resembles coarse crumbs.

Add Water:

- Gradually add ice water, a few tablespoons at a time, and mix until the dough comes together. Be careful not to overwork the dough.

Form a Disk:

- Shape the dough into a disk, wrap it in plastic wrap, and refrigerate for at least 30 minutes.

Prepare the Filling:

Cook Beef:

- In a skillet over medium heat, cook the ground beef until browned. Drain excess fat if necessary.

Sauté Aromatics:

- Add chopped onions and minced garlic to the skillet and sauté until the onions are translucent.

Season:

- Stir in ground cumin, paprika, dried oregano, salt, and pepper. Add tomato paste and mix well.

Optional Ingredients:

- If using, add chopped green olives and boiled eggs to the beef mixture. Stir until combined.

Cool Filling:

- Allow the beef filling to cool completely.

Assemble and Fry:

Roll Out Dough:

- Preheat the oven to 375°F (190°C).
- Roll out the chilled dough on a floured surface to about 1/8-inch thickness.

Cut Circles:

- Use a round cutter or a glass to cut out circles from the dough.

Fill and Seal:

- Place a spoonful of the beef filling in the center of each dough circle. Fold the dough over the filling to create a half-moon shape. Seal the edges by pressing with a fork.

Fry Empanadas:

- In a deep skillet, heat vegetable oil over medium-high heat. Fry the empanadas in batches until golden brown on both sides, about 2-3 minutes per side.

Drain and Bake:

- Place the fried empanadas on a paper towel to drain excess oil. Transfer them to a baking sheet and bake in the preheated oven for an additional 10 minutes to ensure they are fully cooked and heated through.

Serve:

- Serve the beef empanadas hot as a delicious appetizer or snack.

These beef empanadas can be enjoyed on their own or with your favorite dipping sauces. Feel free to get creative with the fillings, adding ingredients like raisins or peppers for additional flavor.

Beef Empanadas Recipe

Ingredients:

For the Dough:

- 3 cups all-purpose flour
- 1 teaspoon salt
- 1 cup unsalted butter, cold and diced
- 1/2 cup ice water

For the Filling:

- 1 pound ground beef
- 1 onion, finely chopped
- 2 cloves garlic, minced
- 1 teaspoon ground cumin
- 1 teaspoon paprika
- 1/2 teaspoon dried oregano
- Salt and pepper to taste
- 1/4 cup tomato paste
- 1/4 cup green olives, chopped (optional)
- 2 boiled eggs, chopped (optional)
- Vegetable oil for frying

Instructions:

Prepare the Dough:

 Combine Ingredients:
 - In a large bowl, mix the flour and salt. Add the diced cold butter and use your fingers or a pastry cutter to incorporate until the mixture resembles coarse crumbs.

 Add Water:

- Gradually add ice water, a few tablespoons at a time, and mix until the dough comes together. Be careful not to overwork the dough.

Form a Disk:

- Shape the dough into a disk, wrap it in plastic wrap, and refrigerate for at least 30 minutes.

Prepare the Filling:

Cook Beef:

- In a skillet over medium heat, cook the ground beef until browned. Drain excess fat if necessary.

Sauté Aromatics:

- Add chopped onions and minced garlic to the skillet and sauté until the onions are translucent.

Season:

- Stir in ground cumin, paprika, dried oregano, salt, and pepper. Add tomato paste and mix well.

Optional Ingredients:

- If using, add chopped green olives and boiled eggs to the beef mixture. Stir until combined.

Cool Filling:

- Allow the beef filling to cool completely.

Assemble and Fry:

Roll Out Dough:

- Preheat the oven to 375°F (190°C).
- Roll out the chilled dough on a floured surface to about 1/8-inch thickness.

Cut Circles:

- Use a round cutter or a glass to cut out circles from the dough.

Fill and Seal:

- Place a spoonful of the beef filling in the center of each dough circle. Fold the dough over the filling to create a half-moon shape. Seal the edges by pressing with a fork.

Fry Empanadas:

- In a deep skillet, heat vegetable oil over medium-high heat. Fry the empanadas in batches until golden brown on both sides, about 2-3 minutes per side.

Drain and Bake:

- Place the fried empanadas on a paper towel to drain excess oil. Transfer them to a baking sheet and bake in the preheated oven for an additional 10 minutes to ensure they are fully cooked and heated through.

Serve:

- Serve the beef empanadas hot as a delicious appetizer or snack.

These beef empanadas can be enjoyed on their own or with your favorite dipping sauces. Feel free to get creative with the fillings, adding ingredients like raisins or peppers for additional flavor.

Black Bean Quesadillas Recipe

Ingredients:

- 1 can (15 ounces) black beans, drained and rinsed
- 1 cup corn kernels (fresh, frozen, or canned)
- 1 cup shredded Mexican cheese blend (cheddar, Monterey Jack, and/or queso fresco)
- 1/2 cup diced tomatoes
- 1/4 cup diced red onion
- 1/4 cup chopped fresh cilantro
- 1 teaspoon ground cumin
- 1 teaspoon chili powder
- Salt and pepper to taste
- 4 large flour tortillas
- Cooking oil or butter for cooking
- Optional toppings: salsa, guacamole, sour cream

Instructions:

Prepare Black Bean Filling:

- In a mixing bowl, combine black beans, corn, shredded cheese, diced tomatoes, diced red onion, chopped cilantro, ground cumin, chili powder, salt, and pepper. Mix well to ensure even distribution of ingredients.

Assemble Quesadillas:

- Lay out the flour tortillas on a clean surface. Spoon the black bean mixture onto one half of each tortilla, spreading it evenly.

Fold and Press:

- Fold the other half of each tortilla over the filling, creating a half-moon shape. Press down gently to secure the ingredients.

Cook the Quesadillas:

- Heat a skillet or griddle over medium heat. Add a small amount of cooking oil or butter to coat the surface.

- Place the quesadillas in the skillet and cook for 2-3 minutes on each side or until the tortillas are golden brown and the cheese is melted.

Slice and Serve:

- Remove the quesadillas from the skillet and let them cool for a moment. Slice each quesadilla into wedges.

Optional Toppings:

- Serve the black bean quesadillas hot, and if desired, top with salsa, guacamole, or sour cream.

Enjoy:

- Enjoy these delicious black bean quesadillas as a quick and satisfying meal or snack.

Feel free to customize the quesadillas by adding other ingredients such as diced bell peppers, jalapeños, or your favorite spices. They are versatile and make for a great vegetarian option that doesn't compromise on flavor.

Sopes with Chorizo Recipe

Ingredients:

For the Sopes:

- 2 cups masa harina (corn masa flour)
- 1 1/4 cups warm water
- 1/2 teaspoon salt
- Vegetable oil for frying

For the Chorizo Topping:

- 1/2 pound chorizo sausage, casing removed
- 1/2 onion, finely chopped
- 1 clove garlic, minced
- 1 cup refried beans
- Salt and pepper to taste

For Toppings:

- Shredded lettuce
- Diced tomatoes
- Sliced radishes
- Crumbled queso fresco or shredded Mexican cheese blend
- Fresh cilantro, chopped
- Lime wedges

Instructions:

Prepare the Sopes:

Make the Masa Dough:

- In a large bowl, mix masa harina, warm water, and salt until a soft dough forms. Knead the dough for a few minutes until smooth.

Form Small Dough Balls:

- Divide the dough into golf ball-sized portions.

Shape the Sopes:

- Take each ball and flatten it with your hands to form a small, thick disc (about 3 inches in diameter). Create a raised edge around the disc to form a border.

Fry the Sopes:

- Heat vegetable oil in a skillet over medium-high heat. Fry the sopes on both sides until golden brown and cooked through. Place them on paper towels to absorb excess oil.

Prepare the Chorizo Topping:

Cook Chorizo:

- In a separate skillet, cook chorizo over medium heat, breaking it apart with a spatula as it cooks.

Add Aromatics:

- Add finely chopped onion and minced garlic to the chorizo. Cook until the onions are translucent.

Season and Add Beans:

- Season with salt and pepper to taste. Stir in refried beans and cook until the mixture is heated through.

Assemble the Sopes:

Top Sopes:

- Spoon a generous portion of the chorizo and bean mixture onto each sope.

Add Toppings:

- Top the chorizo with shredded lettuce, diced tomatoes, sliced radishes, crumbled queso fresco or shredded cheese, and chopped cilantro.

Serve with Lime Wedges:

- Serve the sopes with lime wedges on the side for squeezing over the top.

Enjoy:

- Enjoy these delicious sopes with chorizo and a variety of toppings.

Sopes with chorizo are a delightful and hearty dish, perfect for sharing with family and friends. The combination of the crispy masa base, flavorful chorizo, and vibrant toppings makes for a satisfying and delicious meal.

Spicy Mango Salsa Recipe

Ingredients:

- 2 ripe mangoes, peeled, pitted, and diced
- 1/2 red onion, finely chopped
- 1 jalapeño pepper, seeds removed and finely chopped
- 1/4 cup fresh cilantro, chopped
- Juice of 2 limes
- 1 tablespoon honey or agave nectar
- Salt and pepper to taste
- Optional: 1/2 red bell pepper, finely diced for added color

Instructions:

Prepare Mangoes:

- Peel, pit, and dice the ripe mangoes. Place the diced mangoes in a mixing bowl.

Chop Ingredients:

- Finely chop the red onion, jalapeño pepper (seeds removed for less heat), and fresh cilantro. If using, finely dice the red bell pepper.

Combine Ingredients:

- Add the chopped red onion, jalapeño, cilantro, and red bell pepper (if using) to the bowl with the diced mangoes.

Make the Dressing:

- In a small bowl, whisk together the lime juice and honey or agave nectar. Pour the dressing over the mango mixture.

Toss and Season:

- Gently toss the ingredients to coat them evenly with the dressing. Season with salt and pepper to taste. Adjust the sweetness or acidity by adding more honey or lime juice if needed.

Chill (Optional):

- For optimal flavor, you can refrigerate the spicy mango salsa for at least 30 minutes before serving to allow the flavors to meld.

Serve:

- Serve the spicy mango salsa as a vibrant topping for grilled chicken, fish, tacos, or as a refreshing dip with tortilla chips.

Enjoy:

- Enjoy the sweet and spicy combination of flavors in this delicious mango salsa!

This spicy mango salsa is versatile and can be customized based on your preferences. You can also experiment with additional ingredients like diced avocado, cucumber, or pineapple for added complexity. It's a great way to add a tropical twist to your meals.

Tostadas with Refried Beans Recipe

Ingredients:

For the Refried Beans:

- 2 cups cooked pinto or black beans (canned or homemade)
- 2 tablespoons vegetable oil
- 1/2 onion, finely chopped
- 2 cloves garlic, minced
- 1 teaspoon ground cumin
- 1 teaspoon chili powder
- Salt and pepper to taste
- 1/2 cup vegetable broth or water (as needed)

For the Tostadas:

- Corn tostada shells (store-bought or homemade)
- Refried beans (prepared using the recipe above)
- Shredded lettuce
- Diced tomatoes
- Sliced radishes
- Crumbled queso fresco or shredded Mexican cheese blend
- Fresh cilantro, chopped
- Sour cream or Mexican crema
- Lime wedges for serving

Instructions:

Prepare Refried Beans:

Sauté Aromatics:

- In a skillet, heat vegetable oil over medium heat. Add finely chopped onion and minced garlic. Sauté until the onions are translucent.

Add Beans and Spices:

- Add cooked beans to the skillet along with ground cumin, chili powder, salt, and pepper. Mash the beans with a potato masher or the back of a spoon.

Cook and Add Liquid:

- Cook the beans, stirring occasionally, until they are heated through. If the mixture is too thick, add vegetable broth or water gradually to achieve the desired consistency.

Adjust Seasoning:

- Taste and adjust the seasoning as needed. Keep the refried beans warm.

Assemble Tostadas:

Prepare Tostada Shells:

- If using store-bought tostada shells, warm them in the oven according to the package instructions. If making homemade tostada shells, fry corn tortillas in hot oil until crispy, then drain on paper towels.

Spread Refried Beans:

- Spread a generous layer of warm refried beans onto each tostada shell.

Add Toppings:

- Top the refried beans with shredded lettuce, diced tomatoes, sliced radishes, crumbled queso fresco or shredded cheese, and chopped cilantro.

Finish with Creamy Toppings:

- Add a dollop of sour cream or Mexican crema on top of each tostada.

Serve with Lime Wedges:

- Serve the tostadas with lime wedges on the side for squeezing over the top.

Enjoy:

- Enjoy these delicious tostadas with refried beans as a flavorful and satisfying meal.

Feel free to customize the toppings based on your preferences. Tostadas with refried beans are versatile and can be a great way to use leftover beans. They make for a tasty and quick meal that's perfect for lunch or dinner.

Mexican Deviled Eggs Recipe

Ingredients:

- 6 hard-boiled eggs, peeled and halved
- 3 tablespoons mayonnaise
- 1 tablespoon Dijon mustard
- 1 tablespoon fresh lime juice
- 1 teaspoon hot sauce (adjust to taste)
- 1/2 teaspoon ground cumin
- Salt and pepper to taste
- 2 tablespoons finely chopped red onion
- 2 tablespoons finely chopped fresh cilantro
- Optional garnish: paprika, chili powder, or additional chopped cilantro

Instructions:

Prepare Hard-Boiled Eggs:

- Hard-boil the eggs, then peel and halve them lengthwise. Remove the yolks and place them in a bowl.

Make the Filling:

- Mash the egg yolks with a fork. Add mayonnaise, Dijon mustard, fresh lime juice, hot sauce, ground cumin, salt, and pepper. Mix well until smooth.

Add Ingredients:

- Stir in finely chopped red onion and fresh cilantro into the yolk mixture. Adjust the seasoning to taste.

Fill the Egg Whites:

- Spoon or pipe the yolk mixture back into the egg white halves, creating a slightly mounded top.

Garnish:

- Garnish each deviled egg with a sprinkle of paprika, chili powder, or additional chopped cilantro for added flavor and presentation.

Chill:
- Refrigerate the Mexican deviled eggs for at least 30 minutes before serving to allow the flavors to meld and the filling to set.

Serve:
- Arrange the Mexican deviled eggs on a serving platter and serve chilled.

These Mexican deviled eggs offer a zesty and spicy twist with the addition of lime juice, hot sauce, cumin, red onion, and cilantro. They make a colorful and flavorful appetizer for parties, gatherings, or as a unique addition to your holiday spread. Enjoy!

Soups and Salads:

Tortilla Soup Recipe

Ingredients:

For the Soup:

- 1 tablespoon vegetable oil
- 1 onion, finely chopped
- 2 cloves garlic, minced
- 1 jalapeño, seeds removed and finely chopped (optional for heat)
- 1 teaspoon ground cumin
- 1 teaspoon chili powder
- 1 can (14 ounces) diced tomatoes
- 1 can (10 ounces) diced tomatoes with green chilies (e.g., Rotel)
- 6 cups chicken broth
- 2 cups shredded cooked chicken
- 1 cup corn kernels (fresh, frozen, or canned)
- 1 cup black beans, drained and rinsed
- Salt and pepper to taste
- Juice of 1 lime

For Garnish:

- Tortilla strips or tortilla chips
- Avocado slices
- Fresh cilantro, chopped
- Shredded cheese (cheddar or Mexican blend)

- Sour cream or Mexican crema
- Lime wedges

Instructions:

Sauté Aromatics:

- In a large pot, heat vegetable oil over medium heat. Add finely chopped onion, minced garlic, and chopped jalapeño (if using). Sauté until the onions are translucent.

Add Spices:

- Stir in ground cumin and chili powder, cooking for an additional minute until fragrant.

Tomato Base:

- Add both cans of diced tomatoes (with their juices) to the pot. Cook for a few minutes to soften the tomatoes.

Simmer:

- Pour in the chicken broth and bring the mixture to a simmer. Let it cook for about 15-20 minutes, allowing the flavors to meld.

Add Chicken and Vegetables:

- Stir in shredded cooked chicken, corn kernels, and black beans. Cook for an additional 10-15 minutes.

Season:

- Season the soup with salt and pepper to taste. Squeeze the juice of one lime into the soup.

Prepare Garnishes:

- While the soup is simmering, prepare the garnishes. Cut tortillas into strips and fry them until crispy, or use store-bought tortilla chips. Gather avocado slices, chopped cilantro, shredded cheese, sour cream, and lime wedges.

Serve:

- Ladle the hot tortilla soup into bowls. Top each serving with tortilla strips, avocado slices, chopped cilantro, shredded cheese, a dollop of sour cream, and a lime wedge.

Enjoy:

- Serve the tortilla soup hot and enjoy the comforting and flavorful bowl of goodness.

Tortilla soup is customizable, so feel free to adjust the spice level, add more vegetables, or include other toppings of your choice. It's a perfect soup for warming up on a chilly day!

Pozole Recipe

Ingredients:

For the Pozole:

- 2 pounds pork shoulder or pork butt, cut into chunks
- 1 large onion, finely chopped
- 4 cloves garlic, minced
- 2 cans (29 ounces each) hominy, drained and rinsed
- 8 cups chicken or pork broth
- 1 teaspoon dried oregano
- 1 teaspoon ground cumin
- Salt and pepper to taste

For the Garnish:

- Radishes, sliced
- Cabbage, shredded
- Avocado, diced
- Fresh cilantro, chopped
- Lime wedges
- Red chili flakes (optional)
- Tortillas or tostadas on the side

Instructions:

Prepare the Pozole:

    Cook the Pork:

- In a large pot, combine the pork chunks, chopped onion, minced garlic, dried oregano, ground cumin, salt, and pepper. Cover with water and bring to a boil. Reduce heat and simmer until the pork is tender, usually 2 to 3 hours.

Shred the Pork:

- Once the pork is cooked, shred it using two forks. You can also use a slotted spoon to remove the pork pieces, shred them, and return them to the pot.

Add Hominy and Broth:

- Add the drained hominy and chicken or pork broth to the pot. Bring the mixture to a simmer and cook for an additional 30 minutes to allow the flavors to meld.

Season:

- Taste and adjust the seasoning with salt and pepper. You can also add more cumin or oregano if desired.

Serve Pozole:

Prepare Garnishes:

- While the pozole is simmering, prepare the garnishes. Slice radishes, shred cabbage, dice avocado, and chop fresh cilantro.

Serve Hot:

- Ladle the hot pozole into bowls. Allow each person to customize their pozole with garnishes according to their preference.

Enjoy:

- Serve the pozole hot with lime wedges and, if desired, red chili flakes for added spice. Enjoy with tortillas or tostadas on the side.

Pozole is often served during celebrations and special occasions, and it's a comforting and flavorful soup that brings people together. Feel free to adjust the recipe based on your preferences and enjoy the rich and hearty flavors of this Mexican classic.

Black Bean Soup Recipe

Ingredients:

- 2 cans (15 ounces each) black beans, drained and rinsed
- 2 tablespoons olive oil
- 1 large onion, chopped
- 2 bell peppers (any color), chopped
- 3 cloves garlic, minced
- 1 teaspoon ground cumin
- 1 teaspoon chili powder
- 1/2 teaspoon smoked paprika
- 1/2 teaspoon dried oregano
- 4 cups vegetable or chicken broth
- 1 can (14 ounces) diced tomatoes
- Salt and black pepper to taste
- Juice of 1 lime
- Optional toppings: chopped fresh cilantro, sour cream, diced avocado, shredded cheese

Instructions:

Sauté Aromatics:

- In a large pot, heat olive oil over medium heat. Add chopped onion and bell peppers. Sauté until the vegetables are softened, about 5 minutes.

Add Garlic and Spices:

- Add minced garlic, ground cumin, chili powder, smoked paprika, and dried oregano to the pot. Stir well and cook for an additional 1-2 minutes until the spices are fragrant.

Combine Black Beans:

- Add one can of black beans to the pot. Use an immersion blender to partially blend the soup, leaving some beans whole for texture. If you don't have an immersion blender, transfer a portion of the soup to a blender, blend, and return it to the pot.

Add Broth and Tomatoes:

- Pour in the vegetable or chicken broth and add the diced tomatoes. Bring the soup to a simmer.

Season:

- Season the soup with salt and black pepper to taste. Adjust the seasoning as needed.

Simmer:

- Allow the soup to simmer for about 15-20 minutes, allowing the flavors to meld and the soup to thicken slightly.

Add Remaining Black Beans:

- Stir in the remaining can of black beans. Let the soup simmer for an additional 5-10 minutes.

Finish with Lime Juice:

- Squeeze the juice of one lime into the soup. Stir well to incorporate.

Serve:

- Ladle the hot black bean soup into bowls. Garnish with chopped fresh cilantro, a dollop of sour cream, diced avocado, or shredded cheese, if desired.

Enjoy:

- Serve the black bean soup hot and enjoy the delicious and comforting flavors.

This black bean soup is not only tasty but also versatile. You can customize it by adding additional vegetables, adjusting the spice level, or incorporating your favorite toppings. It's a hearty and satisfying soup that's perfect for lunch or dinner.

Menudo Recipe

Ingredients:

For the Menudo:

- 2 pounds beef tripe, cleaned and cut into small pieces
- 1 pound beef feet or beef shank, cut into chunks
- 1 onion, finely chopped
- 4 cloves garlic, minced
- 2 cans (29 ounces each) hominy, drained and rinsed
- 8 cups beef broth
- 2 teaspoons dried oregano
- Salt and pepper to taste

For the Red Chili Sauce:

- 4 dried guajillo chilies, stemmed and seeded
- 2 dried ancho chilies, stemmed and seeded
- 3 cups hot water (for soaking chilies)
- 2 tomatoes, roasted
- 1/2 onion, roasted
- 3 cloves garlic, roasted
- 1 teaspoon ground cumin
- 1 teaspoon dried oregano
- Salt to taste

Instructions:

Prepare the Beef Tripe:

Clean and Boil:

- Clean the beef tripe thoroughly, removing any excess fat or membrane. Boil the beef tripe and beef feet in a large pot of water until tender, about 2-3 hours. Discard the water and set the cooked tripe and feet aside.

Prepare the Red Chili Sauce:

Soak Chilies:

- In a bowl, soak the dried guajillo and ancho chilies in hot water for about 15-20 minutes until they soften.

Roast Vegetables:

- While the chilies are soaking, roast the tomatoes, onion, and garlic until they are slightly charred.

Blend the Sauce:

- In a blender, combine the soaked chilies (discard the soaking water), roasted tomatoes, onion, garlic, ground cumin, dried oregano, and salt. Blend until smooth to create the red chili sauce.

Cook the Menudo:

Sauté Aromatics:

- In a large pot, sauté finely chopped onion and minced garlic until translucent.

Add Red Chili Sauce:

- Pour the red chili sauce into the pot and cook for a few minutes until the sauce thickens and the flavors meld.

Add Beef Tripe and Broth:

- Add the boiled beef tripe and beef feet to the pot. Pour in beef broth and add dried oregano. Season with salt and pepper to taste. Bring the mixture to a simmer.

Simmer:

- Allow the menudo to simmer for at least 1-2 hours to allow the flavors to develop.

Add Hominy:

- About 30 minutes before serving, add the drained and rinsed hominy to the pot. Continue simmering until the hominy is heated through.

Adjust Seasoning:

- Taste and adjust the seasoning if needed. Add more salt or pepper to suit your preference.

Serve Menudo:

Ladle into Bowls:

- Ladle the hot menudo into bowls.

Garnish:

- Serve the menudo with lime wedges, diced onions, chopped cilantro, oregano, and crushed red pepper on the side.

Enjoy:

- Enjoy this classic Mexican menudo with its rich and spicy flavors.

Menudo is often enjoyed as a comforting soup, especially during special occasions and celebrations. It is also believed to have potential health benefits and is sometimes referred to as a "hangover cure." Adjust the spice level and garnishes according to your taste preferences.

Ensalada de Nopales (Cactus Salad) Recipe

Ingredients:

- 2 cups fresh nopales (cactus pads), cleaned and diced
- 1 tomato, diced
- 1/2 red onion, finely chopped
- 1/2 cup fresh cilantro, chopped
- 1 jalapeño, seeds removed and finely chopped (optional)
- 2 tablespoons olive oil
- Juice of 2 limes
- Salt and pepper to taste
- Queso fresco or feta cheese, crumbled (optional)
- Avocado slices for garnish (optional)

Instructions:

Prepare Nopales:

- Clean the nopales by removing the spines and edges. Dice the nopales into bite-sized pieces.

Cook Nopales:

- Bring a pot of water to a boil. Add the diced nopales and cook for about 8-10 minutes until they are tender but still firm. Drain and let them cool.

Assemble Salad:

- In a large bowl, combine the cooked nopales with diced tomato, chopped red onion, fresh cilantro, and chopped jalapeño if using.

Make Dressing:

- In a small bowl, whisk together olive oil, lime juice, salt, and pepper to create the dressing.

Dress the Salad:

- Pour the dressing over the salad ingredients and toss gently to coat everything evenly.

Chill (Optional):
- If time allows, refrigerate the salad for at least 30 minutes to let the flavors meld.

Garnish:
- If desired, garnish the salad with crumbled queso fresco or feta cheese and avocado slices.

Serve:
- Serve the Ensalada de Nopales chilled or at room temperature.

Enjoy:
- Enjoy this cactus salad as a refreshing side dish or as a topping for tacos and other Mexican dishes.

Ensalada de nopales is not only delicious but also packed with health benefits. Nopales are low in calories, high in fiber, and rich in vitamins and minerals. The combination of flavors in this salad makes it a delightful and unique addition to your culinary repertoire.

Esquites (Mexican Street Corn Salad) Recipe

Ingredients:

- 4 cups corn kernels (freshly grilled or boiled)
- 1/4 cup mayonnaise
- 1/4 cup sour cream or Mexican crema
- 1/2 cup crumbled cotija cheese
- 1 teaspoon chili powder (adjust to taste)
- 1/2 teaspoon smoked paprika
- 1 clove garlic, minced
- Juice of 1 lime
- Salt and pepper to taste
- Fresh cilantro, chopped, for garnish
- Optional: Tajin seasoning for extra spice
- Optional: Hot sauce (e.g., Valentina or Tapatio)

Instructions:

Prepare Corn:

- Grill or boil the corn kernels until they are cooked. If grilling, you can leave the corn on the cob and then cut the kernels off.

Make Dressing:

- In a small bowl, whisk together mayonnaise, sour cream or Mexican crema, minced garlic, lime juice, chili powder, smoked paprika, salt, and pepper.

Combine Corn and Dressing:

- In a large mixing bowl, combine the cooked corn kernels with the dressing. Toss until the corn is well coated.

Add Cotija Cheese:

- Sprinkle crumbled cotija cheese over the corn and gently toss to incorporate.

Adjust Seasoning:

- Taste the esquites and adjust the seasoning as needed. You can add more salt, pepper, or chili powder according to your preference.

Optional Spice:

- If you like additional spice, sprinkle Tajin seasoning over the esquites and mix. You can also add hot sauce for an extra kick.

Garnish:

- Garnish the esquites with chopped fresh cilantro.

Serve:

- Serve the Mexican street corn salad in individual cups or bowls.

Enjoy:

- Enjoy the delicious flavors of esquites as a side dish or a snack. It's a perfect accompaniment to grilled meats or as a topping for tacos.

Esquites is a popular street food in Mexico, and it captures the essence of elote (Mexican street corn) in a convenient salad form. The combination of creamy dressing, tangy cotija cheese, and the smoky flavors of chili powder make this dish a crowd-pleaser.

Chicken Avocado Lime Soup Recipe

Ingredients:

- 1 tablespoon olive oil
- 1 onion, finely chopped
- 2 cloves garlic, minced
- 1 pound boneless, skinless chicken breasts, cut into bite-sized pieces
- 6 cups chicken broth
- 2 tomatoes, diced
- 1 jalapeño, seeds removed and finely chopped
- 1 teaspoon ground cumin
- 1 teaspoon chili powder
- Salt and pepper to taste
- Juice of 2 limes
- 2 avocados, peeled, pitted, and diced
- Fresh cilantro, chopped, for garnish
- Tortilla strips or chips for serving (optional)
- Sour cream or Mexican crema for serving (optional)

Instructions:

Sauté Aromatics:

- In a large pot, heat olive oil over medium heat. Add chopped onion and minced garlic. Sauté until the onions are translucent.

Cook Chicken:

- Add the chicken pieces to the pot and cook until they are browned on all sides.

Add Broth and Vegetables:

- Pour in the chicken broth and add diced tomatoes, chopped jalapeño, ground cumin, chili powder, salt, and pepper. Bring the soup to a simmer.

Simmer:

- Allow the soup to simmer for about 15-20 minutes until the chicken is cooked through and the flavors meld.

Lime Juice:

- Stir in the lime juice to the soup, adjusting the acidity to your liking. Taste and adjust the seasoning if needed.

Add Avocado:

- Just before serving, gently stir in the diced avocados. Be careful not to over-stir to maintain the avocado's texture.

Garnish:

- Garnish the soup with chopped fresh cilantro.

Serve:

- Ladle the Chicken Avocado Lime Soup into bowls. If desired, top with tortilla strips or chips and a dollop of sour cream or Mexican crema.

Enjoy:

- Enjoy this refreshing and flavorful chicken avocado lime soup.

This soup is not only delicious but also customizable. You can add additional toppings such as shredded cheese, diced red onion, or a sprinkle of chili flakes for extra heat. It's a perfect light and satisfying soup, especially during warmer seasons.

Cilantro Lime Rice Salad Recipe

Ingredients:

- 2 cups cooked white or brown rice (cooled)
- 1/4 cup fresh cilantro, chopped
- 2 tablespoons fresh lime juice
- 1 tablespoon olive oil
- 1 clove garlic, minced
- 1/4 teaspoon ground cumin
- Salt and pepper to taste
- 1 cup cherry tomatoes, halved
- 1/2 cup cucumber, diced
- 1/4 cup red onion, finely chopped
- 1/4 cup bell pepper (any color), diced
- Optional: 1 jalapeño, seeds removed and finely chopped for heat
- Optional: 1/2 cup black beans, drained and rinsed
- Optional: 1/4 cup corn kernels (fresh, frozen, or canned)

Instructions:

Prepare Rice:

- Cook the rice according to package instructions. Once cooked, let it cool to room temperature.

Make Dressing:

- In a small bowl, whisk together lime juice, olive oil, minced garlic, ground cumin, salt, and pepper to create the dressing.

Combine Rice and Dressing:

- In a large bowl, combine the cooled rice with the dressing. Toss to coat the rice evenly.

Add Vegetables:

- Add chopped cilantro, cherry tomatoes, diced cucumber, finely chopped red onion, diced bell pepper, and jalapeño (if using) to the bowl. Gently toss to combine.

Optional Additions:

- If desired, add black beans and corn kernels to the salad. Mix well.

Chill (Optional):

- For optimal flavor, you can refrigerate the cilantro lime rice salad for at least 30 minutes before serving to allow the flavors to meld.

Serve:

- Serve the cilantro lime rice salad as a refreshing side dish alongside grilled chicken, fish, shrimp, or as a component of a burrito bowl.

Enjoy:

- Enjoy the vibrant flavors of cilantro and lime in this delightful rice salad.

Feel free to customize the recipe based on your preferences. You can also add diced avocado, mango, or pineapple for a tropical twist. This cilantro lime rice salad is versatile, light, and perfect for bringing a burst of flavor to your meals.

Mexican Caesar Salad Recipe

Ingredients:

For the Caesar Dressing:

- 1/2 cup mayonnaise
- 2 tablespoons grated Parmesan cheese
- 1 tablespoon Dijon mustard
- 2 cloves garlic, minced
- 2 anchovy fillets, mashed (or 1-2 teaspoons anchovy paste)
- 2 tablespoons fresh lime juice
- 1 teaspoon Worcestershire sauce
- Salt and pepper to taste

For the Salad:

- Romaine lettuce, washed and chopped
- Tortilla strips (store-bought or homemade)
- 1 cup cherry tomatoes, halved
- 1/2 cup crumbled queso fresco or cotija cheese
- Avocado slices
- Fresh cilantro, chopped, for garnish
- Lime wedges for serving

Instructions:

Prepare the Caesar Dressing:

> Combine Ingredients:

- In a bowl, whisk together mayonnaise, grated Parmesan cheese, Dijon mustard, minced garlic, mashed anchovy fillets (or anchovy paste), lime juice, and Worcestershire sauce.

Season:

- Taste the dressing and add salt and pepper according to your preference. Keep in mind that the anchovies and Parmesan cheese contribute saltiness to the dressing.

Assemble the Mexican Caesar Salad:

Prepare Romaine Lettuce:

- Wash and chop the Romaine lettuce into bite-sized pieces.

Toss with Dressing:

- In a large bowl, toss the chopped Romaine lettuce with the prepared Caesar dressing until evenly coated.

Add Toppings:

- Add halved cherry tomatoes, tortilla strips, crumbled queso fresco or cotija cheese, and avocado slices to the salad.

Garnish:

- Garnish the Mexican Caesar salad with chopped fresh cilantro.

Serve:

- Serve the salad on individual plates or in a large salad bowl.

Top with Lime Wedges:

- Serve the Mexican Caesar salad with lime wedges on the side for squeezing over the top.

Enjoy:

- Enjoy the Mexican Caesar salad as a delicious and satisfying meal or as a side dish to complement your favorite Mexican-inspired dishes.

This Mexican Caesar salad provides a wonderful blend of flavors, combining the richness of the Caesar dressing with the freshness of the lettuce, tomatoes, and the crunch of tortilla strips. It's a perfect addition to your repertoire of salads with a South-of-the-Border flair.

Caldo de Res (Beef Vegetable Soup) Recipe

Ingredients:

For the Broth:

- 2 pounds beef shank or beef stew meat, bone-in
- 1 large onion, quartered
- 3 cloves garlic, peeled
- 2 bay leaves
- Salt to taste
- Water

For the Soup:

- 2 large carrots, sliced
- 2 corn on the cob, each cut into 3-4 pieces
- 2 potatoes, peeled and diced
- 2 zucchinis, sliced
- 1 chayote, peeled and diced
- 1/2 cabbage, chopped
- 3 tomatoes, diced
- 1 cup green beans, trimmed and cut into bite-sized pieces
- 1/2 cup rice
- 1 tablespoon vegetable oil
- Salt and pepper to taste
- Fresh cilantro, chopped, for garnish
- Lime wedges for serving

Instructions:

Prepare the Broth:

Boil the Beef:
- In a large pot, combine beef shank or stew meat, quartered onion, peeled garlic cloves, bay leaves, and a generous pinch of salt. Add enough water to cover the ingredients.

Simmer:
- Bring the pot to a boil and then reduce the heat to simmer. Skim off any foam that rises to the surface.

Cook Until Tender:
- Allow the beef to simmer for at least 1.5 to 2 hours or until the meat is tender. Add more water if needed during cooking.

Strain the Broth:
- Once the beef is tender, strain the broth, discarding the solids. Set aside the cooked beef.

Prepare the Soup:

Sauté Vegetables:
- In a separate pot, heat vegetable oil over medium heat. Sauté the diced tomatoes until they release their juices.

Add Broth and Vegetables:
- Pour in the strained beef broth into the pot with sautéed tomatoes. Add the sliced carrots, corn pieces, diced potatoes, sliced zucchinis, diced chayote, chopped cabbage, green beans, and rice.

Season:

- Season the soup with salt and pepper to taste. Bring the mixture to a boil, then reduce the heat to simmer.

Cook Until Vegetables are Tender:

- Allow the soup to simmer until the vegetables are tender and the rice is cooked.

Add Cooked Beef:

- Shred or cut the cooked beef into bite-sized pieces and add it back to the pot.

Adjust Seasoning:

- Taste and adjust the seasoning as needed. Add more salt and pepper if desired.

Garnish:

- Garnish the Caldo de Res with chopped fresh cilantro.

Serve:

- Serve the Caldo de Res hot with lime wedges on the side for squeezing over the soup.

Caldo de Res is a wholesome and nutritious soup that brings together a variety of vegetables and tender beef in a flavorful broth. It's a complete meal in a bowl and perfect for warming up on chilly days.

Main Dishes - Meat:

Carne Asada Tacos Recipe

Ingredients:

For the Carne Asada:

- 1 1/2 to 2 pounds flank steak or skirt steak
- 1/4 cup soy sauce
- 1/4 cup orange juice
- 1/4 cup lime juice
- 3 cloves garlic, minced
- 1 jalapeño, seeds removed and finely chopped
- 1/4 cup chopped fresh cilantro
- 1 teaspoon ground cumin
- 1 teaspoon chili powder
- 1 teaspoon paprika
- Salt and black pepper to taste

For Serving:

- Corn or flour tortillas, warmed
- Salsa or pico de gallo
- Guacamole or sliced avocados
- Chopped fresh cilantro
- Diced onions
- Lime wedges

Instructions:

Prepare the Marinade:

> Combine Marinade Ingredients:
> - In a bowl, whisk together soy sauce, orange juice, lime juice, minced garlic, chopped jalapeño, chopped cilantro, ground cumin, chili powder, paprika, salt, and black pepper.
>
> Marinate the Steak:

- Place the flank steak or skirt steak in a shallow dish or a resealable plastic bag. Pour the marinade over the steak, ensuring it's well-coated. Marinate in the refrigerator for at least 1-2 hours, or preferably overnight for enhanced flavor.

Grill the Carne Asada:

Preheat the Grill:
- Preheat your grill to medium-high heat.

Grill the Steak:
- Remove the steak from the marinade and let any excess drip off. Grill the steak for about 5-7 minutes per side or until it reaches your desired level of doneness. Cooking times may vary depending on the thickness of the steak.

Rest and Slice:
- Allow the grilled steak to rest for a few minutes, then slice it thinly against the grain.

Assemble the Tacos:

Warm Tortillas:
- Warm the tortillas on the grill or in a skillet.

Assemble Tacos:
- Fill each tortilla with slices of carne asada.

Add Toppings:
- Top the carne asada with salsa or pico de gallo, guacamole or sliced avocados, chopped fresh cilantro, diced onions, and a squeeze of lime juice.

Serve:
- Serve the Carne Asada Tacos immediately and enjoy!

Carne Asada Tacos are perfect for gatherings, parties, or a delicious weeknight dinner. The grilled and seasoned beef, combined with fresh toppings, creates a burst of flavor in every bite. Customize your tacos with your favorite toppings and enjoy the vibrant and delicious taste of authentic Carne Asada Tacos.

Chicken Mole Recipe

Ingredients:

For the Mole Sauce:

- 3 dried ancho chilies, stemmed and seeded
- 3 dried guajillo chilies, stemmed and seeded
- 2 dried pasilla chilies, stemmed and seeded
- 1/4 cup raisins
- 1/4 cup almonds
- 2 tablespoons sesame seeds
- 2 tablespoons vegetable oil
- 1 medium onion, chopped
- 3 cloves garlic, minced
- 1/2 teaspoon ground cinnamon
- 1/4 teaspoon ground cloves
- 1/4 teaspoon ground cumin
- 1/4 teaspoon dried oregano
- 1/4 teaspoon ground coriander
- 1/4 teaspoon ground anise
- 1/4 cup masa harina (corn flour)
- 4 cups chicken broth
- 2 ounces unsweetened chocolate, chopped
- Salt and pepper to taste

For the Chicken:

- 3 pounds chicken pieces (whole chicken, drumsticks, thighs, or breasts)

- Salt and pepper to season
- 2 tablespoons vegetable oil

Instructions:

Prepare the Mole Sauce:

  Prepare Chilies:
  - Toast the dried ancho, guajillo, and pasilla chilies in a dry skillet over medium heat until fragrant. Soak them in hot water for about 20 minutes to soften.

  Toast Raisins, Almonds, and Sesame Seeds:
  - In the same skillet, toast raisins, almonds, and sesame seeds until lightly browned. Set aside.

  Sauté Onion and Garlic:
  - In a large saucepan, heat vegetable oil over medium heat. Sauté chopped onion and minced garlic until softened.

  Blend the Sauce:
  - In a blender, combine the soaked and drained chilies, toasted raisins, almonds, sesame seeds, sautéed onion and garlic, ground cinnamon, ground cloves, ground cumin, dried oregano, ground coriander, ground anise, and masa harina. Blend until smooth.

  Make the Mole Sauce:
  - In the same saucepan, pour the blended mixture. Cook over medium heat, stirring constantly, until it thickens and darkens in color.

  Add Chicken Broth and Chocolate:

- Gradually add chicken broth, stirring constantly to avoid lumps. Add the chopped unsweetened chocolate and continue to stir until the chocolate is fully melted.

Simmer:

- Simmer the mole sauce for about 20-30 minutes, stirring occasionally. Season with salt and pepper to taste.

Cook the Chicken:

Season Chicken:

- Season the chicken pieces with salt and pepper.

Sear Chicken:

- In a large skillet or Dutch oven, heat vegetable oil over medium-high heat. Sear the chicken pieces until browned on all sides.

Combine Chicken and Mole Sauce:

- Add the seared chicken to the simmering mole sauce. Cover and let it cook over low heat for about 45 minutes to 1 hour or until the chicken is fully cooked and tender.

Serve:

- Serve the Chicken Mole over rice, accompanied by warm tortillas or crusty bread.

Chicken Mole is a complex and rich dish that marries the sweetness of chocolate with the warmth of various spices. It's a special dish often enjoyed during celebrations and gatherings. Customize the spice level and adjust the consistency of the sauce to your liking. Enjoy the unique and indulgent flavors of this classic Mexican dish.

Barbacoa Recipe

Ingredients:

For the Barbacoa Marinade:

- 3–4 pounds beef cheek, beef chuck, or lamb, cut into large chunks
- 3 cloves garlic, minced
- 1 onion, finely chopped
- 2-3 chipotle peppers in adobo sauce (adjust to taste)
- 1 tablespoon ground cumin
- 1 tablespoon dried oregano
- 1 teaspoon ground cloves
- 1 teaspoon ground cinnamon
- 1/2 cup apple cider vinegar
- Juice of 2 limes
- Salt and black pepper to taste

For Cooking:

- Banana leaves or agave leaves (optional)
- 1 cup beef or vegetable broth
- Corn tortillas for serving
- Chopped onions and fresh cilantro for garnish
- Lime wedges for serving

Instructions:

Prepare the Marinade:

Blend Marinade Ingredients:

- In a blender, combine minced garlic, chopped onion, chipotle peppers, ground cumin, dried oregano, ground cloves, ground cinnamon, apple cider vinegar, lime juice, salt, and black pepper. Blend until you have a smooth marinade.

Marinate the Meat:

- Place the beef or lamb chunks in a large bowl or resealable plastic bag. Pour the marinade over the meat, making sure each piece is well coated. Marinate in the refrigerator for at least 4 hours or overnight for the best flavor.

Cook the Barbacoa:

Preheat Oven or Slow Cooker:

- Preheat your oven to 325°F (163°C) or set your slow cooker to the low setting.

Line Cooking Vessel (Optional):

- If using banana leaves or agave leaves, briefly pass them over an open flame to soften. Line the bottom of your oven-safe pot or slow cooker with the leaves.

Place Meat in Pot:

- Place the marinated meat into the pot or slow cooker, along with any remaining marinade.

Add Broth:

- Pour the beef or vegetable broth over the meat.

Cook:

- If using an oven, cover the pot and place it in the preheated oven. Cook for 3 to 4 hours or until the meat is tender and easily falls apart. If using a slow cooker, cover and cook on low for 6-8 hours or until the meat is tender.

Shred Meat:

- Once cooked, shred the meat using two forks. It should be very tender and flavorful.

Serve Barbacoa:

Serve in Tortillas:

- Serve the shredded barbacoa in warm corn tortillas.

Garnish:

- Garnish with chopped onions, fresh cilantro, and a squeeze of lime juice.

Enjoy:

- Enjoy your Barbacoa tacos with your favorite toppings and salsas.

Barbacoa is a versatile dish that can be enjoyed in tacos, burritos, or on its own with rice and beans. The slow-cooking process allows the meat to absorb the rich flavors of the marinade, resulting in a tender and delicious dish. Adjust the level of spiciness by adding more or fewer chipotle peppers according to your preference.

Carnitas Recipe

Ingredients:

For the Pork:

- 4-5 pounds pork shoulder (or pork butt), cut into large chunks
- 1 onion, quartered
- 4 cloves garlic, smashed
- 1 orange, cut into quarters
- 1 lime, cut into quarters
- 2 bay leaves
- 1 cinnamon stick
- Salt and black pepper to taste
- 2 tablespoons vegetable oil

For the Spice Rub:

- 1 tablespoon ground cumin
- 1 tablespoon dried oregano
- 1 tablespoon chili powder
- 1 tablespoon smoked paprika
- 1 teaspoon ground coriander
- 1 teaspoon ground cloves
- 1 teaspoon salt
- 1/2 teaspoon black pepper

Instructions:

Prepare the Pork:

Season Pork:
- In a large bowl, combine the pork chunks with the spice rub ingredients: ground cumin, dried oregano, chili powder, smoked paprika, ground coriander, ground cloves, salt, and black pepper. Mix well to coat the pork evenly.

Marinate:
- Let the seasoned pork marinate for at least 30 minutes or refrigerate overnight for more flavor.

Cook the Carnitas:

Preheat Oven:
- Preheat your oven to 325°F (163°C).

Sear Pork:
- In a large oven-safe pot or Dutch oven, heat vegetable oil over medium-high heat. Sear the marinated pork chunks until they are browned on all sides.

Add Aromatics:
- Add the quartered onion, smashed garlic cloves, orange quarters, lime quarters, bay leaves, and cinnamon stick to the pot with the seared pork.

Braise:
- Pour enough water into the pot to cover the pork about halfway. Cover the pot and transfer it to the preheated oven.

Slow Cook:
- Slow-cook the pork in the oven for approximately 2.5 to 3 hours or until the pork is tender and easily shreds with a fork.

Shred and Crisp:

- Remove the pot from the oven. Using two forks, shred the pork directly in the pot. If desired, you can transfer the shredded pork to a baking sheet and broil for a few minutes to crisp up the edges.

Serve:

- Serve the carnitas in tacos, burritos, or any other desired dishes.

Optional Step: Crisping in a Skillet (Alternative to Broiling):

Crisp in a Skillet:

- Heat a skillet over medium-high heat. Add a bit of oil, and transfer a portion of shredded carnitas to the skillet. Press the pork down with a spatula and let it crisp up on one side before flipping.

Serve Crispy Carnitas:

- Serve the crispy carnitas on a platter or in tacos, and enjoy!

Carnitas are often served with diced onions, chopped cilantro, lime wedges, and your favorite salsa or hot sauce. The combination of slow-cooking and then crisping the pork results in tender, flavorful, and slightly crispy carnitas that are perfect for a variety of Mexican-inspired dishes.

Cochinita Pibil Recipe

Ingredients:

For the Achiote Marinade:

- 3 tablespoons achiote paste
- 1 teaspoon ground cumin
- 1 teaspoon ground allspice
- 1 teaspoon dried oregano
- 1 teaspoon ground cinnamon
- 4 cloves garlic, minced
- 1/2 cup orange juice
- 1/4 cup white vinegar
- Juice of 2 limes
- Salt to taste

For the Cochinita Pibil:

- 3-4 pounds pork shoulder, cut into chunks
- Banana leaves (optional, for wrapping)
- 1 red onion, thinly sliced
- 2 oranges, sliced
- 1 lime, sliced
- 1/4 cup vegetable oil
- Salt to taste

Instructions:

Prepare the Achiote Marinade:

Combine Ingredients:

- In a bowl, combine the achiote paste, ground cumin, ground allspice, dried oregano, ground cinnamon, minced garlic, orange juice, white vinegar, lime juice, and salt. Mix well to form a smooth marinade.

Marinate the Pork:

Coat Pork:

- Place the pork chunks in a large bowl or resealable plastic bag. Pour the achiote marinade over the pork, ensuring each piece is well coated. Marinate in the refrigerator for at least 4 hours or preferably overnight.

Cook Cochinita Pibil:

Preheat Oven:

- Preheat your oven to 325°F (163°C).

Line Baking Dish:

- If you're not using banana leaves, you can line a baking dish with aluminum foil.

Prepare Banana Leaves (Optional):

- If using banana leaves, briefly pass them over an open flame to soften. Line the baking dish with the banana leaves, letting the edges hang over the sides.

Layer Ingredients:

- Place the marinated pork in the baking dish or on top of the banana leaves. Top with sliced red onion, orange slices, lime slices, and drizzle with vegetable oil. Add salt to taste.

Wrap and Cook:

- If using banana leaves, fold the leaves over the pork to create a package. Cover the baking dish tightly with foil.

Bake:

- Bake in the preheated oven for approximately 3 to 4 hours or until the pork is tender and easily shreds with a fork.

Serve:

- Serve the Cochinita Pibil in tacos, tortas, or on its own. Garnish with additional red onion, cilantro, and lime wedges.

Cochinita Pibil is often served with pickled red onions, fresh cilantro, and warm tortillas. The slow-cooking process in the achiote marinade imparts a rich and flavorful taste to the pork, making it a classic and beloved dish in Mexican cuisine.

Beef Birria Recipe

Ingredients:

For the Birria Marinade:

- 3-4 pounds beef stew meat (such as chuck roast or brisket), cut into chunks
- 3 dried ancho chilies, stemmed and seeded
- 3 dried guajillo chilies, stemmed and seeded
- 2 dried pasilla chilies, stemmed and seeded
- 4 cloves garlic, minced
- 1 onion, chopped
- 1 tablespoon ground cumin
- 1 tablespoon dried oregano
- 1 teaspoon ground coriander
- 1 teaspoon ground cloves
- 1 teaspoon ground cinnamon
- 1 teaspoon salt, or to taste
- 1/2 teaspoon black pepper
- 2 bay leaves
- 1 cup apple cider vinegar
- 2 cups beef broth (or water)

For Cooking the Birria:

- 2 tablespoons vegetable oil
- 3 cups beef broth (or water)
- 1-2 bay leaves
- Salt and pepper to taste

For Serving:

- Corn tortillas
- Chopped fresh cilantro
- Diced onions
- Lime wedges

Instructions:

Prepare the Birria Marinade:

Prepare Chilies:

- Toast the dried ancho, guajillo, and pasilla chilies in a dry skillet over medium heat until fragrant. Soak them in hot water for about 20 minutes to soften.

Blend Marinade Ingredients:

- In a blender, combine the soaked and drained chilies with minced garlic, chopped onion, ground cumin, dried oregano, ground coriander, ground cloves, ground cinnamon, salt, black pepper, bay leaves, apple cider vinegar, and beef broth. Blend until you have a smooth marinade.

Marinate the Meat:

- Place the beef chunks in a large bowl or resealable plastic bag. Pour the marinade over the beef, ensuring each piece is well coated. Marinate in the refrigerator for at least 4 hours or overnight for enhanced flavor.

Cook the Birria:

Preheat Oven:

- Preheat your oven to 325°F (163°C).

Sear the Meat:

- In a large, oven-safe pot or Dutch oven, heat vegetable oil over medium-high heat. Sear the marinated beef chunks until browned on all sides.

Add Cooking Liquid:

- Pour 3 cups of beef broth (or water) into the pot. Add 1-2 bay leaves. Season with additional salt and pepper to taste.

Cover and Slow Cook:

- Cover the pot and transfer it to the preheated oven. Slow-cook for about 3 to 4 hours or until the beef is tender and easily shreds with a fork.

Serve:

- Serve the Beef Birria in tacos, consommé-style (with a side of broth), or as desired.

To Serve Birria Tacos:

Prepare Tacos:

- Heat corn tortillas and fill them with shredded beef from the birria.

Garnish:

- Garnish the tacos with chopped fresh cilantro, diced onions, and a squeeze of lime juice.

Serve:

- Serve the Birria Tacos with lime wedges on the side.

Birria is a flavorful and comforting dish that has gained popularity worldwide. Whether enjoyed in tacos or as a stew, the tender and aromatic beef makes it a delicious and satisfying option for any occasion. Customize your toppings and enjoy the rich flavors of this traditional Mexican dish.

Tacos al Pastor Recipe

Ingredients:

For the Al Pastor Marinade:

- 3–4 pounds pork shoulder, thinly sliced
- 3 dried guajillo chilies, stemmed and seeded
- 3 dried ancho chilies, stemmed and seeded
- 4 cloves garlic, minced
- 1 small onion, chopped
- 1/4 cup white vinegar
- 1/4 cup pineapple juice
- 1 tablespoon achiote paste
- 1 teaspoon ground cumin
- 1 teaspoon dried oregano
- 1 teaspoon smoked paprika
- 1 teaspoon salt, or to taste
- 1/2 teaspoon black pepper
- 1/2 teaspoon ground cinnamon
- 1/4 teaspoon ground cloves
- 1/4 cup vegetable oil

For Cooking and Serving:

- Corn tortillas
- Pineapple, thinly sliced
- Chopped fresh cilantro
- Diced onions

- Lime wedges

Instructions:

Prepare the Al Pastor Marinade:

Prepare Chilies:
- Toast the dried guajillo and ancho chilies in a dry skillet over medium heat until fragrant. Soak them in hot water for about 20 minutes to soften.

Blend Marinade Ingredients:
- In a blender, combine the soaked and drained chilies with minced garlic, chopped onion, white vinegar, pineapple juice, achiote paste, ground cumin, dried oregano, smoked paprika, salt, black pepper, ground cinnamon, ground cloves, and vegetable oil. Blend until you have a smooth marinade.

Marinate the Pork:
- Place the thinly sliced pork shoulder in a large bowl. Pour the al pastor marinade over the pork, ensuring each slice is well coated. Marinate in the refrigerator for at least 4 hours or overnight for the best flavor.

Cook Tacos al Pastor:

Preheat Grill or Oven:
- Preheat your grill or oven to medium-high heat.

Thread Pork Slices:
- Thread the marinated pork slices onto a vertical spit or skewers. If using a grill, you can also place the slices directly on the grates.

Cook on Spit or Grill:

- Cook the pork on the spit or grill, turning occasionally, until the edges are crispy and the pork is fully cooked. This should take approximately 15-20 minutes.

Slice the Meat:

- Once cooked, thinly slice the al pastor pork.

Assemble Tacos al Pastor:

Warm Tortillas:

- Heat the corn tortillas until warm and pliable.

Fill Tortillas:

- Fill each tortilla with slices of al pastor pork.

Add Toppings:

- Top the tacos with sliced pineapple, chopped fresh cilantro, and diced onions.

Serve:

- Serve the Tacos al Pastor with lime wedges on the side.

Tacos al Pastor are often served with a side of grilled pineapple, adding a sweet and tangy element to the savory and spiced pork. Enjoy the tacos with your favorite toppings and salsas for a delicious and authentic Mexican street food experience.

Tinga de Pollo Recipe

Ingredients:

For the Shredded Chicken:

- 2 pounds boneless, skinless chicken breasts or thighs
- 1 onion, halved
- 2 cloves garlic, smashed
- Salt and pepper to taste
- Water for boiling

For the Tinga Sauce:

- 2 tablespoons vegetable oil
- 1 onion, thinly sliced
- 2 cloves garlic, minced
- 2 cups tomato puree or crushed tomatoes
- 2-3 chipotle peppers in adobo sauce, chopped (adjust to taste)
- 1 teaspoon dried oregano
- 1 teaspoon ground cumin
- 1/2 teaspoon smoked paprika
- Salt and pepper to taste
- 1 cup chicken broth (from boiling the chicken)
- 1 bay leaf

For Serving:

- Corn tortillas

- Chopped fresh cilantro
- Diced onions
- Lime wedges
- Crumbled queso fresco or cotija cheese (optional)
- Sliced radishes (optional)
- Avocado slices (optional)

Instructions:

Prepare the Shredded Chicken:

Boil Chicken:

- In a large pot, place the chicken breasts or thighs along with halved onion, smashed garlic, salt, and pepper. Cover with water.

Boil Until Cooked:

- Bring the water to a boil, then reduce heat and simmer until the chicken is fully cooked and easily shreds, about 20-25 minutes.

Shred Chicken:

- Remove the chicken from the pot and shred it using two forks. Reserve 1 cup of the chicken broth for the Tinga sauce.

Prepare the Tinga Sauce:

Sauté Onions and Garlic:

- In a large skillet or pan, heat vegetable oil over medium heat. Sauté thinly sliced onions until softened, then add minced garlic and cook for an additional minute.

Add Tomato Sauce and Spices:

- Pour in the tomato puree or crushed tomatoes, chopped chipotle peppers, dried oregano, ground cumin, smoked paprika, salt, and pepper. Mix well.

Simmer:
- Allow the sauce to simmer for about 10 minutes, allowing the flavors to meld.

Add Shredded Chicken:
- Add the shredded chicken to the sauce, along with 1 cup of the reserved chicken broth. Stir to combine.

Add Bay Leaf:
- Add a bay leaf to the mixture for added flavor.

Simmer Again:
- Let the tinga simmer for an additional 10-15 minutes, or until the sauce thickens and the chicken absorbs the flavors.

Serve Tinga de Pollo:

Warm Tortillas:
- Heat the corn tortillas until warm and pliable.

Fill Tortillas:
- Fill each tortilla with a generous portion of Tinga de Pollo.

Garnish:
- Garnish with chopped fresh cilantro, diced onions, lime wedges, and any optional toppings such as crumbled queso fresco or cotija cheese, sliced radishes, and avocado.

Serve:

- Serve the Tinga de Pollo tacos immediately and enjoy the delicious combination of smoky, spicy chicken with the freshness of garnishes.

Tinga de Pollo is a versatile dish that brings together the bold flavors of chipotle, tomatoes, and spices. It's perfect for taco nights or any occasion where you want to savor the authentic taste of Mexican cuisine.

Chiles en Nogada Recipe

Ingredients:

For the Stuffed Poblano Peppers:

- 6 large poblano peppers
- 1 pound ground beef or pork
- 1/2 cup diced onion
- 2 cloves garlic, minced
- 1/2 cup diced tomatoes
- 1/4 cup raisins
- 1/4 cup sliced almonds
- 1/4 teaspoon ground cinnamon
- 1/4 teaspoon ground cloves
- Salt and pepper to taste
- 2 tablespoons vegetable oil for cooking

For the Walnut Cream Sauce:

- 1 cup walnuts, shelled
- 1 cup queso fresco or mild feta cheese
- 1 cup Mexican crema or sour cream
- 1/2 cup milk
- Salt to taste

For Garnish:

- Seeds from 1 pomegranate

- Fresh parsley, finely chopped

Instructions:

Prepare the Poblano Peppers:

Roast and Peel Poblanos:

- Roast the poblano peppers over an open flame or under a broiler until the skin is charred. Place the roasted peppers in a plastic bag to steam for about 15 minutes. Peel off the skin, make a slit down one side, and remove the seeds.

Prepare the Stuffed Filling:

Cook Ground Meat:

- In a skillet, heat vegetable oil over medium heat. Add diced onion and minced garlic, sauté until softened. Add ground meat and cook until browned.

Add Ingredients:

- Add diced tomatoes, raisins, sliced almonds, ground cinnamon, ground cloves, salt, and pepper. Cook for a few minutes until the flavors meld. Adjust seasoning to taste.

Stuff Poblano Peppers:

- Carefully stuff each poblano pepper with the meat filling. Close the slit using toothpicks or kitchen twine.

Prepare the Walnut Cream Sauce:

Blend Walnut Cream Sauce:

- In a blender, combine shelled walnuts, queso fresco or feta cheese, Mexican crema or sour cream, and milk. Blend until you have a smooth cream sauce. Add salt to taste.

Assemble Chiles en Nogada:

Plate the Stuffed Poblanos:

- Place the stuffed poblano peppers on individual serving plates.

Pour Walnut Cream Sauce:

- Pour the walnut cream sauce over the stuffed poblanos, covering them generously.

Garnish:

- Sprinkle pomegranate seeds and finely chopped fresh parsley on top of the walnut cream sauce.

Serve Chiles en Nogada:

Chill and Serve:

- Chiles en Nogada can be served cold or at room temperature. Chill for a couple of hours before serving to enhance the flavors.

Enjoy:

- Serve Chiles en Nogada as a festive and flavorful dish, perfect for special occasions.

Chiles en Nogada is not only a delicious and visually stunning dish but also a symbol of Mexican culinary heritage. The combination of savory and sweet flavors, along with the richness of the walnut cream sauce, makes it a unique and memorable dish for celebrations.

Salsa Roja Chicken Enchiladas Recipe

Ingredients:

For the Salsa Roja:

- 4 large tomatoes, chopped
- 2-3 dried guajillo chilies, stemmed and seeded
- 2 dried ancho chilies, stemmed and seeded
- 1 small onion, chopped
- 2 cloves garlic, minced
- 1 teaspoon dried oregano
- 1 teaspoon ground cumin
- Salt and pepper to taste
- 2 tablespoons vegetable oil

For the Chicken Filling:

- 2 cups cooked and shredded chicken
- 1 small onion, finely chopped
- 2 cloves garlic, minced
- 1 teaspoon ground cumin
- 1 teaspoon chili powder
- Salt and pepper to taste
- 1 cup shredded Monterey Jack or Mexican blend cheese

For Assembling the Enchiladas:

- 10-12 corn tortillas
- 1 cup shredded cheese for topping

- Fresh cilantro, chopped, for garnish (optional)
- Mexican crema or sour cream for serving (optional)

Instructions:

Prepare the Salsa Roja:

Toast and Soak Chilies:

- Toast the dried guajillo and ancho chilies in a dry skillet over medium heat until fragrant. Soak them in hot water for about 20 minutes to soften.

Blend Salsa Ingredients:

- In a blender, combine the soaked and drained chilies with chopped tomatoes, chopped onion, minced garlic, dried oregano, ground cumin, salt, and pepper. Blend until you have a smooth salsa.

Cook Salsa:

- Heat vegetable oil in a saucepan over medium heat. Pour the blended salsa into the saucepan and simmer for about 10-15 minutes until it thickens. Adjust seasoning if necessary.

Prepare the Chicken Filling:

Sauté Onions and Garlic:

- In a skillet, sauté finely chopped onion and minced garlic until softened.

Add Chicken and Seasonings:

- Add the shredded chicken to the skillet. Season with ground cumin, chili powder, salt, and pepper. Mix well and cook for a few minutes until the flavors meld.

Add Cheese:

- Stir in the shredded cheese and let it melt into the chicken mixture. Remove from heat.

Assemble the Enchiladas:

Preheat Oven:
- Preheat your oven to 350°F (175°C).

Warm Tortillas:
- Heat the corn tortillas in a dry skillet or on a griddle until they are pliable.

Fill and Roll:
- Spoon a portion of the chicken filling onto each tortilla. Roll them up and place them seam-side down in a baking dish.

Pour Salsa Roja:
- Pour the prepared Salsa Roja over the rolled enchiladas, ensuring they are fully covered.

Top with Cheese:
- Sprinkle additional shredded cheese on top of the enchiladas.

Bake:
- Bake in the preheated oven for about 20 minutes or until the cheese is melted and bubbly.

Serve:

Garnish and Serve:
- Remove from the oven and garnish with chopped cilantro if desired. Serve the Salsa Roja Chicken Enchiladas with Mexican crema or sour cream on the side.

These Salsa Roja Chicken Enchiladas are delicious, comforting, and perfect for a family dinner or gathering. Customize the level of spiciness in the salsa to suit your taste, and feel free to add your favorite toppings such as avocado slices, diced tomatoes, or sliced jalapeños. Enjoy!

Beef Tamales Recipe

Ingredients:

For the Beef Filling:

- 1 pound beef chuck or brisket, cooked and shredded
- 1 onion, finely chopped
- 2 cloves garlic, minced
- 1 teaspoon ground cumin
- 1 teaspoon chili powder
- 1 teaspoon dried oregano
- Salt and pepper to taste
- 1 cup beef broth

For the Masa (Dough):

- 2 cups masa harina (corn masa flour)
- 1 cup beef or vegetable broth (warm)
- 1 cup lard or vegetable shortening
- 1 teaspoon baking powder
- 1 teaspoon salt

For Assembling the Tamales:

- Corn husks, soaked in warm water
- 1 cup red salsa (optional, for serving)

Instructions:

Prepare the Beef Filling:

Cook Beef:

- Cook the beef chuck or brisket until tender. This can be done by simmering in water or broth until the meat is easily shredded. Shred the cooked beef.

Sauté Onion and Garlic:

- In a skillet, sauté finely chopped onion and minced garlic until softened.

Add Seasonings:

- Add ground cumin, chili powder, dried oregano, salt, and pepper to the onion and garlic. Stir well.

Combine with Shredded Beef:

- Mix the seasoned onion and garlic mixture with the shredded beef. Add 1 cup of beef broth and simmer until the flavors meld. Adjust seasoning if needed. Set aside.

Prepare the Masa:

Mix Masa Ingredients:

- In a large bowl, combine masa harina, warm beef or vegetable broth, lard or vegetable shortening, baking powder, and salt. Mix well until you have a smooth dough.

Assemble the Tamales:

Prepare Corn Husks:

- Soak corn husks in warm water for about 30 minutes until they are pliable.

Spread Masa on Husks:

- Take a soaked corn husk and spread a thin layer of masa onto the wide end of the husk, leaving about a 1-inch border at the edges.

Add Beef Filling:

- Spoon a portion of the beef filling onto the center of the masa.

Fold and Tie:

- Fold the sides of the corn husk over the filling, then fold the bottom and top to encase the filling completely. Tie the tamale with a strip of soaked corn husk.

Repeat:

- Repeat the process until all masa and filling are used.

Steam the Tamales:

Prepare Steamer:

- Set up a steamer by placing a steaming basket over simmering water. Arrange the tamales vertically in the steamer, open end facing up.

Steam:

- Steam the tamales for about 1.5 to 2 hours or until the masa is firm and fully cooked.

Serve:

Cool and Unwrap:

- Allow the tamales to cool slightly before unwrapping.

Serve with Salsa:

- Optionally, serve the beef tamales with red salsa on the side.

Enjoy these delicious Beef Tamales as a hearty and satisfying meal. They are perfect for celebrations, gatherings, or any time you want to savor the flavors of traditional Mexican cuisine.

Mexican Picadillo Recipe

Ingredients:

- 1 pound ground beef
- 1 tablespoon vegetable oil
- 1 onion, finely chopped
- 2 cloves garlic, minced
- 1 bell pepper, finely chopped
- 2 tomatoes, chopped
- 2 potatoes, peeled and diced
- 1/2 cup raisins
- 1/4 cup sliced green olives
- 2 tablespoons tomato paste
- 1 teaspoon ground cumin
- 1 teaspoon ground coriander
- 1 teaspoon dried oregano
- 1/2 teaspoon ground cinnamon
- Salt and pepper to taste
- 1/2 cup beef or vegetable broth
- Fresh cilantro, chopped (for garnish, optional)

Instructions:

Cook Ground Beef:

- In a large skillet or frying pan, brown the ground beef over medium heat.

Break it apart with a spatula as it cooks. Drain excess fat if necessary.

Sauté Onions and Garlic:

- Add vegetable oil to the skillet. Add finely chopped onions and minced garlic. Sauté until the onions are translucent.

Add Bell Pepper:

- Add the finely chopped bell pepper to the skillet and cook until it becomes tender.

Incorporate Tomatoes:

- Stir in the chopped tomatoes and cook until they release their juices.

Add Potatoes:

- Add the diced potatoes to the mixture and cook for a few minutes until they start to soften.

Season the Picadillo:

- Mix in the tomato paste, ground cumin, ground coriander, dried oregano, ground cinnamon, salt, and pepper. Stir well to coat the ingredients with the spices.

Incorporate Raisins and Olives:

- Add the raisins and sliced green olives to the skillet. Mix them into the picadillo.

Pour Broth:

- Pour the beef or vegetable broth into the skillet. Stir and bring the mixture to a simmer.

Simmer:

- Reduce the heat to low, cover the skillet, and let the picadillo simmer for about 15-20 minutes or until the potatoes are fully cooked and the flavors meld.

Adjust Seasoning:

- Taste and adjust the seasoning with more salt and pepper if needed.

Garnish and Serve:

- Garnish the picadillo with chopped fresh cilantro, if desired. Serve the picadillo as a filling for tacos, empanadas, or alongside rice.

Enjoy the rich and savory flavors of Mexican Picadillo, a comforting and versatile dish that's sure to be a hit at your table.

Camarones a la Diabla Recipe

Ingredients:

For the Shrimp:

- 1 pound large shrimp, peeled and deveined
- 2 tablespoons olive oil
- 4 cloves garlic, minced
- Salt and pepper to taste
- Lime wedges for serving

For the Diabla Sauce:

- 4 dried guajillo chilies, stemmed and seeded
- 2 dried arbol chilies, stemmed and seeded (adjust to taste for spiciness)
- 2 tomatoes, chopped
- 1/2 onion, chopped
- 4 cloves garlic, minced
- 1/2 teaspoon dried oregano
- 1/2 teaspoon ground cumin
- 1/2 teaspoon smoked paprika
- 1 cup chicken or shrimp broth
- 2 tablespoons vegetable oil
- Salt to taste

Instructions:

Prepare the Diabla Sauce:

Soak Chilies:

- In a bowl, soak the dried guajillo and arbol chilies in hot water for about 20 minutes to soften them.

Blend the Sauce:

- In a blender, combine the soaked chilies, chopped tomatoes, chopped onion, minced garlic, dried oregano, ground cumin, smoked paprika, and chicken or shrimp broth. Blend until you have a smooth sauce.

Strain the Sauce:

- Strain the blended sauce through a fine mesh sieve to remove any solids, creating a smooth and silky sauce.

Cook the Shrimp:

Sauté Garlic:

- In a large skillet or pan, heat olive oil over medium heat. Add minced garlic and sauté until fragrant.

Cook Shrimp:

- Add the peeled and deveined shrimp to the skillet. Season with salt and pepper. Cook for 2-3 minutes or until the shrimp just begin to turn pink.

Add Diabla Sauce:

- Pour the prepared Diabla sauce over the shrimp. Stir to coat the shrimp in the spicy sauce.

Simmer:

- Allow the shrimp to simmer in the sauce for another 3-5 minutes or until fully cooked and opaque.

Adjust Seasoning:

- Taste the sauce and adjust the seasoning with salt as needed.

Serve:

Plate and Garnish:

- Serve the Camarones a la Diabla over rice or with warm tortillas. Garnish with lime wedges.

Camarones a la Diabla is known for its bold and spicy flavor profile. Adjust the quantity of arbol chilies according to your desired level of heat. This dish is perfect for those who enjoy a fiery kick in their seafood. Serve it with rice or tortillas to soak up the delicious sauce. Enjoy the heat!

Chicken Tinga Tostadas Recipe

Ingredients:

For the Chicken Tinga:

- 2 cups cooked and shredded chicken (rotisserie chicken works well)
- 1 onion, thinly sliced
- 2 cloves garlic, minced
- 1 can (14 ounces) diced tomatoes
- 2-3 chipotle peppers in adobo sauce, chopped (adjust to taste)
- 1 teaspoon dried oregano
- 1 teaspoon ground cumin
- Salt and pepper to taste
- 2 tablespoons vegetable oil

For the Tostadas:

- Corn tostadas (store-bought or homemade)
- Refried beans
- Shredded lettuce
- Diced tomatoes
- Crumbled queso fresco or cotija cheese
- Fresh cilantro, chopped
- Lime wedges for serving

Instructions:

Prepare the Chicken Tinga:

Sauté Onion and Garlic:

- In a large skillet, heat vegetable oil over medium heat. Add thinly sliced onion and minced garlic. Sauté until the onions are softened.

Add Chipotle Peppers:

- Add chopped chipotle peppers in adobo sauce to the skillet. Stir to combine with the onions and garlic.

Blend Tomatoes:

- In a blender, puree the diced tomatoes until smooth. Add the tomato puree to the skillet.

Season the Sauce:

- Add dried oregano, ground cumin, salt, and pepper to the sauce. Mix well and let it simmer for a few minutes.

Add Shredded Chicken:

- Add the cooked and shredded chicken to the skillet. Coat the chicken with the tinga sauce and let it simmer for 10-15 minutes to absorb the flavors.

Assemble the Chicken Tinga Tostadas:

Spread Refried Beans:

- Spread a layer of refried beans onto each tostada.

Top with Chicken Tinga:

- Spoon the Chicken Tinga over the refried beans on each tostada.

Add Toppings:

- Top the Chicken Tinga with shredded lettuce, diced tomatoes, crumbled queso fresco or cotija cheese, and chopped fresh cilantro.

Serve:

- Serve the Chicken Tinga Tostadas with lime wedges on the side.

Enjoy these Chicken Tinga Tostadas as a vibrant and flavorful meal. The smoky and spicy tinga chicken pairs perfectly with the crunchy tostadas and a variety of fresh toppings. Customize the toppings according to your preferences, and savor the delicious combination of textures and flavors.

Alambre

Ingredients:

For the Alambre Skewers:

- 1 pound beef sirloin or skirt steak, thinly sliced
- 1 onion, thinly sliced
- 1 bell pepper, thinly sliced
- 1 to 2 jalapeño peppers, thinly sliced (optional for added heat)
- 8–10 slices of bacon, cut into small pieces
- 1 cup grated Oaxaca cheese or melting cheese of your choice
- Corn or flour tortillas, for serving

For the Marinade:

- 1/4 cup olive oil
- 2 cloves garlic, minced
- 2 tablespoons fresh lime juice
- 1 teaspoon ground cumin
- 1 teaspoon dried oregano
- Salt and pepper to taste

For Garnish (optional):

- Chopped fresh cilantro
- Salsa or pico de gallo
- Guacamole or sliced avocado

Instructions:

Prepare the Marinade:

Combine Ingredients:

- In a bowl, whisk together the olive oil, minced garlic, fresh lime juice, ground cumin, dried oregano, salt, and pepper.

Marinate the Beef:

- Place the thinly sliced beef in a dish and pour the marinade over it. Ensure that the beef is well-coated. Let it marinate for at least 30 minutes to allow the flavors to infuse.

Assemble and Grill the Alambre Skewers:

Preheat Grill or Grill Pan:

- Preheat your grill or grill pan to medium-high heat.

Skewer the Ingredients:

- Thread the marinated beef, onion slices, bell pepper slices, jalapeño slices (if using), and bacon pieces onto skewers, alternating the ingredients.

Grill the Skewers:

- Grill the skewers for about 8-10 minutes, turning occasionally, until the beef is cooked to your liking and the bacon is crispy.

Add Cheese:

- In the last few minutes of grilling, sprinkle the grated Oaxaca cheese or melting cheese over the skewers, allowing it to melt.

Warm Tortillas:

- While the skewers are grilling, warm the tortillas on the grill or in a separate pan.

Serve Alambre:

Serve on Tortillas:

- Remove the skewers from the grill and carefully slide the ingredients onto warm tortillas.

Garnish:

- Garnish with chopped fresh cilantro and serve with salsa or pico de gallo and guacamole or sliced avocado on the side.

Enjoy Alambre as a tasty and satisfying dish with a variety of textures and flavors. The combination of grilled meats, vegetables, bacon, and melted cheese makes it a favorite for those who love Mexican street food. Serve it as a filling for tacos or enjoy it on its own!

Main Dishes - Vegetarian:

Vegetarian Enchiladas Recipe

Ingredients:

For the Filling:

- 1 tablespoon olive oil
- 1 onion, finely chopped
- 2 bell peppers, diced (any color)
- 1 zucchini, diced
- 1 cup corn kernels (fresh or frozen)
- 1 can (15 ounces) black beans, drained and rinsed
- 1 teaspoon ground cumin
- 1 teaspoon chili powder
- Salt and pepper to taste
- 1 cup shredded cheese (cheddar, Monterey Jack, or a blend)
- 8 large flour or corn tortillas

For the Enchilada Sauce:

- 2 tablespoons olive oil
- 2 tablespoons all-purpose flour
- 2 tablespoons chili powder
- 1 teaspoon ground cumin
- 1/2 teaspoon garlic powder
- 1/4 teaspoon dried oregano
- 2 cups vegetable broth
- Salt to taste

Optional Toppings:

- Chopped fresh cilantro
- Sliced green onions
- Diced tomatoes
- Avocado slices
- Sour cream or Greek yogurt

Instructions:

Prepare the Filling:

Sauté Vegetables:
- In a large skillet, heat olive oil over medium heat. Add chopped onion, diced bell peppers, and diced zucchini. Sauté until the vegetables are softened.

Add Corn and Beans:
- Add corn kernels and black beans to the skillet. Stir in ground cumin, chili powder, salt, and pepper. Cook for a few more minutes until the mixture is well-combined and heated through.

Assemble Filling:
- Remove the skillet from heat and stir in shredded cheese until melted. The cheese will help bind the filling.

Prepare the Enchilada Sauce:

Make Roux:
- In a saucepan, heat olive oil over medium heat. Add flour, chili powder, ground cumin, garlic powder, and dried oregano. Stir to create a roux.

Whisk in Broth:
- Gradually whisk in vegetable broth, ensuring there are no lumps. Cook the sauce over medium heat until it thickens. Add salt to taste.

Simmer:
- Simmer the enchilada sauce for a few minutes until it reaches a smooth and pourable consistency. Adjust seasoning if needed.

Assemble the Enchiladas:

Preheat Oven:
- Preheat your oven to 375°F (190°C).

Prepare Baking Dish:
- Spread a small amount of enchilada sauce in the bottom of a baking dish.

Fill and Roll:
- Spoon the vegetable and cheese filling onto each tortilla, roll it up, and place it seam-side down in the baking dish.

Pour Sauce:
- Pour the remaining enchilada sauce over the rolled tortillas.

Bake:

- Bake in the preheated oven for about 20-25 minutes, or until the enchiladas are heated through, and the edges are slightly crispy.

Serve:

Garnish and Serve:
- Garnish the vegetarian enchiladas with chopped fresh cilantro, sliced green onions, diced tomatoes, avocado slices, and a dollop of sour cream or Greek yogurt if desired.

Enjoy these flavorful Vegetarian Enchiladas as a delicious and satisfying meat-free option. The combination of colorful vegetables, beans, and melted cheese, all wrapped in a flavorful enchilada sauce, makes for a delightful and comforting dish.

Rajas con Crema Recipe

Ingredients:

- 4 large poblano peppers
- 1 tablespoon vegetable oil
- 1 large onion, thinly sliced
- 2 cloves garlic, minced
- 1 cup corn kernels (fresh or frozen)
- 1 cup Mexican crema or sour cream
- 1 cup shredded Oaxaca or Monterey Jack cheese
- Salt and pepper to taste
- Fresh cilantro, chopped (for garnish, optional)
- Warm tortillas for serving

Instructions:

Roast and Peel Poblano Peppers:

Roast the Poblanos:
- Roast the poblano peppers over an open flame, on a grill, or under the broiler until the skin is charred and blistered. Place the roasted peppers in a plastic bag or covered bowl for about 15 minutes to steam.

Peel and Seed:
- Peel the charred skin off the poblano peppers. Remove the seeds and membranes. Slice the poblano peppers into thin strips.

Prepare Rajas con Crema:

Sauté Onions and Garlic:
- In a large skillet, heat vegetable oil over medium heat. Add thinly sliced onions and minced garlic. Sauté until the onions are softened and translucent.

Add Poblano Strips:
- Add the sliced poblano peppers to the skillet. Stir and cook for a few minutes until the peppers are well combined with the onions and garlic.

Incorporate Corn:
- Stir in corn kernels and cook for an additional 2-3 minutes until the corn is heated through.

Add Crema:

- Pour Mexican crema or sour cream into the skillet. Stir well to coat the vegetables. Allow the mixture to simmer for 5-7 minutes, allowing the flavors to meld.

Add Cheese:
- Sprinkle shredded Oaxaca or Monterey Jack cheese over the rajas con crema. Stir until the cheese is melted and the mixture becomes creamy.

Season:
- Season with salt and pepper to taste. Adjust the seasoning as needed.

Serve Rajas con Crema:

Garnish and Serve:
- Garnish with chopped fresh cilantro if desired. Serve the rajas con crema as a side dish or as a filling for warm tortillas.

Enjoy:

- Rajas con Crema is ready to be enjoyed. Serve it with warm tortillas or as a side dish alongside your favorite Mexican meal.

This dish showcases the smoky flavor of roasted poblano peppers, the sweetness of corn, and the richness of crema, creating a delightful combination of textures and flavors. It's a versatile dish that can be customized to suit your taste and preferences.

Veggie Fajitas Recipe

Ingredients:

For the Fajita Seasoning:

- 1 teaspoon chili powder
- 1 teaspoon cumin
- 1 teaspoon paprika
- 1/2 teaspoon onion powder
- 1/2 teaspoon garlic powder
- 1/4 teaspoon cayenne pepper (adjust to taste for spiciness)
- Salt and pepper to taste

For the Veggie Filling:

- 2 tablespoons vegetable oil
- 1 large onion, thinly sliced
- 1 bell pepper, thinly sliced (use a mix of colors for variety)
- 1 zucchini, thinly sliced
- 1 yellow squash, thinly sliced
- 1 cup cherry tomatoes, halved
- 1 cup portobello mushrooms, sliced
- 1 tablespoon soy sauce or tamari (optional, for umami flavor)

For Serving:

- Warm flour or corn tortillas
- Guacamole
- Salsa
- Sour cream or Greek yogurt
- Shredded cheese
- Fresh cilantro, chopped
- Lime wedges

Instructions:

Prepare the Fajita Seasoning:

   Mix Spices:

- In a small bowl, mix together chili powder, cumin, paprika, onion powder, garlic powder, cayenne pepper, salt, and pepper. This is your fajita seasoning.

Sauté Veggie Filling:

Heat Oil:
- In a large skillet or pan, heat vegetable oil over medium-high heat.

Sauté Onion and Bell Pepper:
- Add thinly sliced onion and bell pepper to the skillet. Sauté for 2-3 minutes until they start to soften.

Add Zucchini and Yellow Squash:
- Add thinly sliced zucchini and yellow squash to the skillet. Continue to sauté for an additional 3-4 minutes until the vegetables are tender-crisp.

Incorporate Mushrooms and Tomatoes:
- Add sliced portobello mushrooms and halved cherry tomatoes to the skillet. Cook for another 2-3 minutes until the mushrooms release their juices.

Season with Fajita Seasoning:
- Sprinkle the fajita seasoning over the sautéed vegetables. Add soy sauce or tamari if using. Toss the vegetables to coat them evenly with the seasoning.

Cook Until Tender:
- Continue cooking for an additional 2-3 minutes until the vegetables are fully cooked but still vibrant and slightly crisp.

Serve Veggie Fajitas:

Warm Tortillas:
- Heat the tortillas according to package instructions.

Assemble Fajitas:
- Spoon the sautéed veggie filling onto warm tortillas.

Add Toppings:
- Top with guacamole, salsa, sour cream or Greek yogurt, shredded cheese, and chopped fresh cilantro.

Garnish and Serve:
- Garnish with lime wedges and serve the veggie fajitas immediately.

Enjoy:

- These Veggie Fajitas are a vibrant and flavorful meal that captures the essence of Mexican cuisine. Customize the toppings to your liking and savor the delicious combination of seasoned vegetables wrapped in warm tortillas.

Spinach and Mushroom Quesadillas Recipe

Ingredients:

- 8 medium-sized flour tortillas
- 2 cups baby spinach, chopped
- 1 cup mushrooms, sliced
- 1 small onion, finely chopped
- 2 cloves garlic, minced
- 1 cup shredded Monterey Jack or mozzarella cheese
- 1 tablespoon olive oil
- Salt and pepper to taste
- Optional toppings: salsa, guacamole, sour cream, chopped cilantro

Instructions:

Sauté Mushrooms and Onions:
- In a skillet, heat olive oil over medium heat. Add chopped onions and sliced mushrooms. Sauté until the mushrooms release their moisture and the onions become translucent.

Add Spinach:
- Add minced garlic and chopped baby spinach to the skillet. Sauté for an additional 2-3 minutes until the spinach wilts. Season with salt and pepper to taste.

Assemble Quesadillas:
- On a separate skillet or griddle, place one tortilla. Spread a portion of the spinach and mushroom mixture evenly over half of the tortilla. Sprinkle shredded cheese on top.

Fold and Cook:
- Fold the other half of the tortilla over the filling, creating a half-moon shape. Press down with a spatula and cook for 2-3 minutes on each side, or until the tortilla is golden brown and the cheese is melted.

Repeat:
- Repeat the process for the remaining tortillas, adjusting the filling and cheese quantities accordingly.

Slice and Serve:
- Once the quesadillas are cooked, remove them from the skillet and let them rest for a minute. Slice each quesadilla into wedges.

Optional Toppings:

- Serve the spinach and mushroom quesadillas with your choice of toppings, such as salsa, guacamole, sour cream, or chopped cilantro.

Enjoy:
- Enjoy these delicious and nutritious Spinach and Mushroom Quesadillas as a quick and flavorful meal.

Feel free to customize these quesadillas by adding other ingredients like diced tomatoes, black beans, or corn. The combination of sautéed spinach, mushrooms, and melted cheese in a warm tortilla makes for a delightful and satisfying dish.

Chiles Rellenos de Queso Recipe

Ingredients:

For the Chiles Rellenos:

- 4 large poblano peppers
- 2 cups queso fresco or shredded Monterey Jack cheese
- 1 cup all-purpose flour (for coating)
- Vegetable oil (for frying)

For the Egg Batter:

- 4 large eggs, separated
- 1/4 teaspoon salt
- 1 cup all-purpose flour

For the Tomato Sauce (optional):

- 2 cups diced tomatoes
- 1/2 onion, chopped
- 2 cloves garlic, minced
- 1/2 teaspoon dried oregano
- Salt and pepper to taste
- 1 tablespoon vegetable oil

Instructions:

Prepare the Poblano Peppers:

Roast and Peel:
- Roast the poblano peppers over an open flame, on a grill, or under the broiler until the skin is charred and blistered. Place them in a plastic bag or covered bowl for about 15 minutes to steam. Peel off the charred skin.

Make a Lengthwise Incision:
- Make a lengthwise incision on each poblano pepper, creating a pocket. Be careful not to cut all the way through.

Remove Seeds:
- Remove the seeds and membranes from inside the peppers.

Stuff with Cheese:

- Stuff each poblano pepper with queso fresco or shredded Monterey Jack cheese, making sure to fill the entire cavity. Close the incision with toothpicks if needed to keep the cheese from oozing out.

Prepare the Egg Batter:

Separate Eggs:
- In a bowl, separate the egg whites from the yolks.

Whip Egg Whites:
- Whip the egg whites with a pinch of salt until stiff peaks form.

Beat Egg Yolks:
- In a separate bowl, beat the egg yolks. Gradually add 1 cup of flour to create a smooth batter.

Fold in Egg Whites:
- Gently fold the whipped egg whites into the yolk and flour mixture until well combined.

Coat and Fry:

Coat Stuffed Peppers:
- Roll each stuffed poblano pepper in flour to coat.

Dip in Egg Batter:
- Dip the coated poblano peppers into the egg batter, making sure they are well-covered.

Fry:
- In a large skillet, heat vegetable oil over medium-high heat. Carefully place the battered peppers in the hot oil and fry until golden brown on all sides.

Drain and Remove Toothpicks:
- Remove the fried peppers from the oil and place them on paper towels to drain excess oil. Remove any toothpicks if used.

Prepare Tomato Sauce (Optional):

Sauté Onions and Garlic:
- In a separate pan, heat vegetable oil and sauté chopped onions and minced garlic until softened.

Add Tomatoes and Seasonings:
- Add diced tomatoes, dried oregano, salt, and pepper. Cook until the tomatoes break down and the sauce thickens.

Serve:

> Plate and Serve:
> - Serve the Chiles Rellenos de Queso on a plate, drizzled with the optional tomato sauce. Remove any remaining toothpicks before serving.

Enjoy these Chiles Rellenos de Queso as a flavorful and satisfying dish, showcasing the richness of melted cheese within the mild poblano peppers.

Vegan Tacos with Chipotle Crema Recipe

Ingredients:

For the Taco Filling:

- 1 can (15 ounces) black beans, drained and rinsed
- 1 cup corn kernels (fresh or frozen)
- 1 medium-sized avocado, diced
- 1 cup cherry tomatoes, halved
- 1/2 red onion, finely chopped
- Fresh cilantro, chopped
- Lime wedges for serving
- Salt and pepper to taste

For the Chipotle Crema:

- 1 cup raw cashews, soaked in hot water for at least 1 hour
- 1 chipotle pepper in adobo sauce (adjust to taste)
- 2 tablespoons adobo sauce (from the can of chipotle peppers)
- 2 tablespoons lime juice
- 1 clove garlic, minced
- 1/2 cup water (adjust for desired consistency)
- Salt to taste

For Assembling Tacos:

- Corn or flour tortillas
- Shredded lettuce or cabbage (optional)

Instructions:

Prepare the Taco Filling:

**In a large bowl, combine drained black beans, corn kernels, diced avocado, cherry tomatoes, red onion, and chopped cilantro.
Season the filling with salt and pepper to taste.
Squeeze fresh lime juice over the mixture and toss everything together.
Set the taco filling aside.

Prepare the Chipotle Crema:

**In a blender, combine soaked cashews, chipotle pepper, adobo sauce, lime juice, minced garlic, and water. Blend until smooth and creamy.
Add more water if needed to achieve your desired consistency.
Season the crema with salt to taste. Adjust chipotle pepper or adobo sauce for more heat if desired.

Assemble the Vegan Tacos:

**Warm the tortillas in a dry skillet or microwave.
Spoon a portion of the taco filling onto each tortilla.
Drizzle the chipotle crema over the filling.
Optionally, add shredded lettuce or cabbage for extra crunch.
Garnish with additional cilantro and serve with lime wedges on the side.

Serve:

Serve the Vegan Tacos with Chipotle Crema immediately and enjoy the flavorful and satisfying plant-based meal.

Feel free to customize the taco filling with your favorite vegan toppings, such as guacamole, salsa, or pickled onions. The chipotle crema adds a creamy and smoky element to these tacos, making them a tasty and satisfying option for a meatless meal.

Zucchini and Corn Tamales Recipe

Ingredients:

For the Corn Masa Dough:

- 2 cups masa harina
- 1 cup vegetable broth
- 1 cup corn kernels (fresh or frozen)
- 1/2 cup vegan butter or vegetable shortening, softened
- 1 teaspoon baking powder
- 1/2 teaspoon salt

For the Zucchini and Corn Filling:

- 2 tablespoons vegetable oil
- 2 zucchini, diced
- 1 cup corn kernels (fresh or frozen)
- 1 small onion, finely chopped
- 2 cloves garlic, minced
- 1 teaspoon ground cumin
- 1/2 teaspoon chili powder
- Salt and pepper to taste

For Assembling the Tamales:

- Corn husks, soaked in warm water for about 30 minutes
- Vegan-friendly tamale wrappers (optional)
- Kitchen twine or strips of soaked corn husks for tying (optional)

Instructions:

Prepare the Corn Masa Dough:

**In a large bowl, combine masa harina, vegetable broth, corn kernels, vegan butter or vegetable shortening, baking powder, and salt.
Mix until a soft dough forms. The consistency should be similar to cookie dough. If needed, add more broth or masa harina to achieve the right texture.
Cover the bowl with a damp cloth and let the masa dough rest while preparing the filling.

Prepare the Zucchini and Corn Filling:

**In a skillet, heat vegetable oil over medium heat. Add chopped onion and cook until softened.
Add minced garlic, diced zucchini, and corn kernels to the skillet.
Season with ground cumin, chili powder, salt, and pepper. Cook until the vegetables are tender but not mushy.
Remove the skillet from heat and set the filling aside.

Assemble the Zucchini and Corn Tamales:

Assemble the Tamales:
- Take a soaked corn husk and spread a thin layer of masa dough in the center, leaving space around the edges.
- Spoon a portion of the zucchini and corn filling onto the masa.

Fold and Tie:
- Fold the sides of the corn husk toward the center, enclosing the filling in the masa dough.
- If using tamale wrappers, fold them around the tamales.
- Tie the tamales with kitchen twine or strips of soaked corn husks to secure them.

Steam the Tamales:
- Place the tamales upright in a steamer basket, ensuring they are tightly packed to prevent unraveling.
- Steam the tamales over medium heat for approximately 1 to 1.5 hours, or until the masa is fully cooked and firm.

Check for Doneness:
- To check for doneness, remove a tamale and let it cool for a few minutes. The masa should easily separate from the husk.

Serve:
- Unwrap the tamales and serve them warm. Optionally, garnish with salsa, guacamole, or vegan sour cream.

Enjoy these Zucchini and Corn Tamales as a flavorful and satisfying dish with a delicious combination of masa, zucchini, and corn. They are perfect for a special occasion or as a comforting meal.

Sweet Potato and Black Bean Burritos Recipe

Ingredients:

For the Sweet Potato Filling:

- 2 medium-sized sweet potatoes, peeled and diced
- 1 tablespoon olive oil
- 1 teaspoon ground cumin
- 1 teaspoon smoked paprika
- Salt and pepper to taste

For the Black Bean Filling:

- 1 can (15 ounces) black beans, drained and rinsed
- 1 small red onion, finely chopped
- 2 cloves garlic, minced
- 1 teaspoon ground cumin
- 1 teaspoon chili powder
- Salt and pepper to taste

For Assembling the Burritos:

- Large flour tortillas
- Cooked brown rice or quinoa
- Salsa or pico de gallo
- Guacamole or sliced avocado
- Shredded lettuce or cabbage
- Vegan cheese (optional)
- Fresh cilantro, chopped (for garnish)
- Lime wedges

Instructions:

Prepare the Sweet Potato Filling:

    Preheat Oven:
- Preheat the oven to 400°F (200°C).

Toss Sweet Potatoes:

- In a bowl, toss the diced sweet potatoes with olive oil, ground cumin, smoked paprika, salt, and pepper until well coated.

Roast Sweet Potatoes:
- Spread the seasoned sweet potatoes on a baking sheet in a single layer. Roast in the preheated oven for 20-25 minutes or until they are tender and slightly crispy, stirring halfway through.

Prepare the Black Bean Filling:

Sauté Onion and Garlic:
- In a skillet, heat olive oil over medium heat. Add chopped red onion and minced garlic. Sauté until the onion is softened.

Add Black Beans and Seasonings:
- Add drained black beans to the skillet. Stir in ground cumin, chili powder, salt, and pepper. Cook for a few minutes until the beans are heated through.

Assemble the Burritos:

Warm Tortillas:
- Heat the flour tortillas according to package instructions.

Layer Ingredients:
- On each tortilla, layer cooked brown rice or quinoa, roasted sweet potatoes, black bean mixture, salsa or pico de gallo, guacamole or sliced avocado, shredded lettuce or cabbage, and vegan cheese if using.

Fold and Roll:
- Fold in the sides of the tortilla and then roll it up tightly to form the burrito.

Serve:
- Place the burritos seam-side down on a serving plate. Garnish with chopped cilantro and serve with lime wedges on the side.

Enjoy these Sweet Potato and Black Bean Burritos as a flavorful and filling meal. Customize the fillings and toppings to suit your taste preferences, and savor the combination of sweet potatoes, black beans, and vibrant, fresh ingredients wrapped in a warm tortilla.

Mexican Quinoa Bowl Recipe

Ingredients:

For the Quinoa:

- 1 cup quinoa, rinsed
- 2 cups vegetable broth or water
- 1 teaspoon ground cumin
- 1/2 teaspoon chili powder
- Salt and pepper to taste

For the Black Bean and Corn Salsa:

- 1 can (15 ounces) black beans, drained and rinsed
- 1 cup corn kernels (fresh or frozen)
- 1 small red onion, finely chopped
- 1 red bell pepper, diced
- 1 jalapeño, finely chopped (seeds removed for less heat)
- 1/4 cup fresh cilantro, chopped
- Juice of 1 lime
- Salt and pepper to taste

For the Avocado Cream Sauce:

- 1 ripe avocado
- 1/4 cup plain Greek yogurt or vegan yogurt
- 1 clove garlic, minced
- 2 tablespoons lime juice
- Salt and pepper to taste
- Water (as needed to adjust consistency)

For Toppings:

- Shredded lettuce or cabbage
- Cherry tomatoes, halved
- Sliced radishes
- Pickled red onions
- Sliced jalapeños
- Fresh cilantro leaves

- Lime wedges

Instructions:

Prepare the Quinoa:

Cook Quinoa:
- In a medium saucepan, combine quinoa, vegetable broth or water, ground cumin, chili powder, salt, and pepper. Bring to a boil, then reduce heat to low, cover, and simmer for about 15-20 minutes, or until quinoa is cooked and liquid is absorbed. Fluff with a fork.

Prepare the Black Bean and Corn Salsa:

Combine Ingredients:
- In a bowl, combine black beans, corn kernels, chopped red onion, diced red bell pepper, chopped jalapeño, cilantro, lime juice, salt, and pepper. Mix well.

Prepare the Avocado Cream Sauce:

Blend Avocado Cream:
- In a blender or food processor, blend together ripe avocado, Greek yogurt or vegan yogurt, minced garlic, lime juice, salt, and pepper until smooth. Add water as needed to achieve the desired sauce consistency.

Assemble the Mexican Quinoa Bowl:

Layer Quinoa:
- Spoon a generous portion of cooked quinoa into serving bowls as the base.

Add Black Bean and Corn Salsa:
- Top the quinoa with the prepared black bean and corn salsa.

Drizzle Avocado Cream Sauce:
- Drizzle the avocado cream sauce over the quinoa and salsa.

Add Toppings:
- Add shredded lettuce or cabbage, halved cherry tomatoes, sliced radishes, pickled red onions, sliced jalapeños, and fresh cilantro leaves on top.

Garnish with Lime Wedges:
- Garnish the bowl with lime wedges for an extra burst of citrus flavor.

Serve:

Serve immediately and enjoy the vibrant and flavorful Mexican Quinoa Bowl!

Feel free to customize the bowl with additional toppings like sliced avocado, vegan cheese, or your favorite hot sauce. This Mexican Quinoa Bowl is a well-balanced and satisfying meal that brings together the goodness of quinoa, black beans, fresh vegetables, and a creamy avocado sauce.

Nopalitos and Potato Tacos Recipe

Ingredients:

For the Nopalitos and Potato Filling:

- 2 medium-sized potatoes, peeled and diced
- 1 cup nopalitos (cactus paddles), cleaned and diced
- 1 small onion, finely chopped
- 2 cloves garlic, minced
- 1 teaspoon ground cumin
- 1 teaspoon chili powder
- Salt and pepper to taste
- 2 tablespoons vegetable oil

For Assembling the Tacos:

- Corn or flour tortillas
- Shredded lettuce or cabbage
- Salsa or pico de gallo
- Guacamole or sliced avocado
- Fresh cilantro, chopped
- Lime wedges

Instructions:

Prepare the Nopalitos and Potato Filling:

Cook Potatoes:
- In a pot of boiling water, cook diced potatoes until they are tender. Drain and set aside.

Prepare Nopalitos:
- Clean the nopalitos by removing thorns and edges. Dice them into small pieces.

Sauté Onion and Garlic:
- In a large skillet, heat vegetable oil over medium heat. Add finely chopped onion and minced garlic. Sauté until the onion is softened.

Add Potatoes and Nopalitos:
- Add the cooked diced potatoes and diced nopalitos to the skillet. Stir to combine.

Season:
- Season the mixture with ground cumin, chili powder, salt, and pepper. Cook for an additional 5-7 minutes, allowing the flavors to meld.

Sauté Until Golden:
- Sauté the potato and nopalitos mixture until the potatoes are golden and the nopalitos are tender.

Assemble the Nopalitos and Potato Tacos:

Warm Tortillas:
- Heat the tortillas in a dry skillet or according to package instructions.

Layer Ingredients:
- On each tortilla, spoon a portion of the nopalitos and potato filling.

Add Toppings:
- Top the filling with shredded lettuce or cabbage, salsa or pico de gallo, guacamole or sliced avocado, and chopped fresh cilantro.

Squeeze Lime:
- Squeeze fresh lime juice over the tacos for added freshness.

Serve:

Serve the Nopalitos and Potato Tacos immediately and enjoy the flavorful and satisfying combination of nopalitos and potatoes in each bite!

These tacos offer a unique and delicious twist with the addition of nopalitos, which have a mild, slightly tangy flavor and a satisfying crunch. Customize the toppings to your liking and savor these Nopalitos and Potato Tacos for a tasty and filling meal.

Side Dishes:

Mexican Rice Recipe

Ingredients:

- 1 cup long-grain white rice
- 1 tablespoon vegetable oil
- 1 small onion, finely chopped
- 2 cloves garlic, minced
- 1 can (14 ounces) diced tomatoes (or 2 cups fresh tomatoes, diced)
- 1 3/4 cups vegetable broth or chicken broth
- 1 teaspoon ground cumin
- 1/2 teaspoon chili powder
- Salt and pepper to taste
- Fresh cilantro, chopped (for garnish, optional)
- Lime wedges (for serving)

Instructions:

Rinse the Rice:
- Rinse the white rice under cold water until the water runs clear. This helps remove excess starch and prevents the rice from becoming too sticky.

Sauté Rice:
- In a large skillet or saucepan, heat the vegetable oil over medium heat. Add the rinsed rice and sauté for 2-3 minutes until the rice becomes lightly golden.

Add Onion and Garlic:
- Add finely chopped onion and minced garlic to the skillet. Sauté for an additional 2-3 minutes until the onion is translucent.

Incorporate Tomatoes:
- Stir in the diced tomatoes (including the juice) and cook for 2 minutes.

Add Broth and Seasonings:
- Pour in the vegetable broth or chicken broth. Add ground cumin, chili powder, salt, and pepper. Stir well to combine.

Simmer and Cover:
- Bring the mixture to a boil, then reduce the heat to low. Cover the skillet or saucepan with a tight-fitting lid and simmer for 15-18 minutes or until the rice is tender and the liquid is absorbed.

Fluff the Rice:
- Once the rice is cooked, fluff it with a fork to separate the grains.

Garnish and Serve:
- If desired, garnish the Mexican rice with chopped fresh cilantro. Serve hot with lime wedges on the side.

Enjoy your homemade Mexican Rice as a flavorful and versatile side dish that pairs well with a variety of Mexican main courses!

Refried Beans Recipe

Ingredients:

- 2 cups cooked pinto beans (canned or freshly cooked)
- 2 tablespoons vegetable oil
- 1/2 cup finely chopped onion
- 2 cloves garlic, minced
- 1 teaspoon ground cumin
- 1/2 teaspoon chili powder
- Salt and pepper to taste
- 1/4 cup water (optional, for adjusting consistency)
- Fresh cilantro, chopped (for garnish, optional)

Instructions:

Cook the Beans:
- If using canned beans, drain and rinse them thoroughly. If using freshly cooked beans, make sure they are tender.

Sauté Onion and Garlic:
- In a large skillet or saucepan, heat vegetable oil over medium heat. Add finely chopped onion and minced garlic. Sauté until the onion is translucent.

Add Beans:
- Add the cooked pinto beans to the skillet. Stir and cook for a few minutes.

Seasoning:
- Season the beans with ground cumin, chili powder, salt, and pepper. Adjust the seasoning to your taste.

Mash the Beans:
- Using a potato masher or the back of a fork, mash the beans to your desired consistency. If you prefer smoother beans, you can use a blender or food processor.

Add Water (Optional):
- If the beans seem too thick, you can add a little water to achieve the desired consistency. Stir well.

Simmer:
- Reduce the heat to low and let the beans simmer for an additional 10-15 minutes, allowing the flavors to meld.

Garnish and Serve:
- If desired, garnish the refried beans with chopped fresh cilantro. Serve hot.

Enjoy your homemade Refried Beans as a side dish, filling for burritos or tacos, or as a dip with tortilla chips! These beans are not only delicious but also versatile, making them a classic and comforting addition to many Mexican meals.

Grilled Street Corn (Elote Asado) Recipe

Ingredients:

- 4 ears of fresh corn, husked
- 1/2 cup mayonnaise
- 1/2 cup crumbled cotija cheese (or feta cheese)
- 1 teaspoon chili powder (adjust to taste)
- 1/2 teaspoon smoked paprika
- 1 clove garlic, minced
- Juice of 1 lime
- Fresh cilantro, chopped (for garnish)
- Lime wedges (for serving)

Instructions:

Grill the Corn:
- Preheat your grill to medium-high heat. Grill the husked corn, turning occasionally, until it has a nice char on all sides. This usually takes about 10-12 minutes.

Prepare the Coating:
- While the corn is grilling, mix the mayonnaise, crumbled cotija cheese, chili powder, smoked paprika, minced garlic, and lime juice in a bowl. Adjust the chili powder to your preferred level of spiciness.

Coat the Grilled Corn:
- Once the corn is done, use a brush or a spoon to coat each ear of corn with the mayo and cheese mixture. Make sure to coat each side evenly.

Garnish:
- Sprinkle the coated corn with additional chili powder and chopped cilantro for extra flavor. The cotija cheese can also be crumbled on top.

Serve:
- Serve the Grilled Street Corn hot, with lime wedges on the side for squeezing over the top.

Enjoy your homemade Grilled Street Corn (Elote Asado) as a delicious and flavorful side dish or snack! This iconic Mexican street food is a perfect balance of smoky, creamy, and tangy flavors.

Sautéed Calabacitas (Mexican Zucchini) Recipe

Ingredients:

- 2 tablespoons vegetable oil
- 1 small onion, finely chopped
- 2 cloves garlic, minced
- 4 medium-sized zucchini, diced
- 1 cup corn kernels (fresh or frozen)
- 1 small tomato, diced
- 1/2 teaspoon ground cumin
- 1/2 teaspoon chili powder
- Salt and pepper to taste
- Fresh cilantro, chopped (for garnish, optional)
- Lime wedges (for serving)

Instructions:

Sauté Onion and Garlic:
- In a large skillet, heat vegetable oil over medium heat. Add finely chopped onion and minced garlic. Sauté until the onion is translucent.

Add Zucchini:
- Add the diced zucchini to the skillet. Cook for about 5-7 minutes, or until the zucchini is slightly tender but still has a bit of crunch.

Incorporate Corn:
- Stir in the corn kernels and continue to cook for an additional 3-4 minutes.

Add Tomato:
- Add the diced tomato to the skillet. Cook for another 2-3 minutes until the tomato is softened.

Season:
- Season the calabacitas with ground cumin, chili powder, salt, and pepper. Adjust the seasoning according to your taste.

Cook Until Tender:
- Continue cooking the calabacitas for an additional 5-7 minutes or until the zucchini is fully tender.

Garnish:
- If desired, garnish the sautéed calabacitas with chopped fresh cilantro.

Serve:
- Serve the calabacitas hot, with lime wedges on the side for squeezing over the top.

Enjoy your homemade Sautéed Calabacitas as a flavorful and vibrant side dish! This dish is versatile and can be served alongside rice, as a taco filling, or as a topping for grilled meats.

Cilantro Lime Rice Recipe

Ingredients:

- 1 cup long-grain white rice
- 2 cups water or vegetable broth
- 1 tablespoon vegetable oil
- 1/2 teaspoon salt
- Zest of 1 lime
- Juice of 2 limes
- 1/4 cup fresh cilantro, finely chopped

Instructions:

Rinse the Rice:
- Rinse the rice under cold water until the water runs clear. This helps remove excess starch and prevents the rice from becoming too sticky.

Cook the Rice:
- In a medium saucepan, heat the vegetable oil over medium heat. Add the rinsed rice and sauté for 1-2 minutes until the rice is lightly toasted.
- Pour in the water or vegetable broth and add salt. Bring the mixture to a boil.
- Reduce the heat to low, cover the saucepan with a tight-fitting lid, and simmer for 15-18 minutes or until the rice is cooked and the liquid is absorbed.

Fluff the Rice:
- Once the rice is cooked, fluff it with a fork to separate the grains.

Add Lime Zest and Juice:
- Add the lime zest and squeeze the juice of two limes over the cooked rice. Stir to combine.

Mix in Cilantro:
- Gently fold in the finely chopped cilantro, distributing it evenly throughout the rice.

Adjust Seasoning:
- Taste the Cilantro Lime Rice and adjust the seasoning if needed, adding more salt or lime juice to suit your preferences.

Serve:
- Serve the Cilantro Lime Rice as a side dish with your favorite Mexican or Southwestern meals.

Enjoy your homemade Cilantro Lime Rice as a zesty and aromatic accompaniment to tacos, burritos, grilled chicken, or other dishes! The combination of fresh cilantro and lime adds a burst of flavor to the rice, making it a delicious and versatile addition to your menu.

Jicama and Mango Salad Recipe

Ingredients:

For the Salad:

- 1 medium-sized jicama, peeled and julienned
- 2 ripe mangoes, peeled, pitted, and diced
- 1 cucumber, peeled and sliced
- 1 red bell pepper, thinly sliced
- 1/2 red onion, thinly sliced
- Fresh cilantro, chopped (for garnish)

For the Dressing:

- Juice of 2 limes
- 2 tablespoons olive oil
- 1 tablespoon honey or agave nectar
- 1 teaspoon ground cumin
- Salt and pepper to taste
- Red chili flakes (optional, for a hint of spice)

Instructions:

Prepare the Salad:

Prep the Ingredients:
- Peel and julienne the jicama.
- Peel, pit, and dice the ripe mangoes.
- Peel and slice the cucumber.
- Thinly slice the red bell pepper and red onion.

Combine Ingredients:
- In a large mixing bowl, combine the jicama, diced mangoes, sliced cucumber, red bell pepper, and red onion.

Prepare the Dressing:

Whisk the Dressing:
- In a small bowl, whisk together the lime juice, olive oil, honey or agave nectar, ground cumin, salt, pepper, and red chili flakes (if using).

Dress the Salad:
- Pour the dressing over the jicama and mango mixture. Toss gently to coat the ingredients evenly.

Chill (Optional):
- If time allows, refrigerate the salad for about 30 minutes to let the flavors meld and the salad to chill.

Garnish and Serve:

Garnish:
- Before serving, garnish the Jicama and Mango Salad with chopped fresh cilantro.

Serve:
- Serve the salad as a refreshing side dish or as a topping for tacos, grilled chicken, or fish.

Enjoy your homemade Jicama and Mango Salad as a light and flavorful addition to your summer meals! The combination of jicama and mango, along with the zesty dressing, creates a deliciously crisp and tropical salad.

Charro Beans Recipe

Ingredients:

- 2 cups dried pinto beans, soaked overnight and drained
- 1 tablespoon vegetable oil
- 1 onion, finely chopped
- 4 cloves garlic, minced
- 1 jalapeño, seeds removed and finely chopped
- 8 slices bacon, chopped
- 1 can (14 ounces) diced tomatoes with juices
- 1/4 cup fresh cilantro, chopped
- 1 teaspoon ground cumin
- 1 teaspoon chili powder
- Salt and pepper to taste
- 4 cups chicken or vegetable broth
- 1 cup water
- 1 bay leaf
- Fresh lime wedges (for serving)

Instructions:

Soak the Pinto Beans:
- Place the dried pinto beans in a large bowl, cover with water, and let them soak overnight. Drain the soaked beans before cooking.

Sauté Aromatics:
- In a large pot or Dutch oven, heat vegetable oil over medium heat. Add finely chopped onion, minced garlic, and chopped jalapeño. Sauté until the vegetables are softened.

Add Bacon:
- Add the chopped bacon to the pot and cook until it starts to brown.

Incorporate Tomatoes and Seasonings:
- Stir in the diced tomatoes with their juices, chopped cilantro, ground cumin, chili powder, salt, and pepper. Cook for a few minutes to allow the flavors to meld.

Add Beans, Broth, and Water:
- Add the soaked and drained pinto beans to the pot. Pour in the chicken or vegetable broth and water. Stir well.

Include Bay Leaf:
- Add a bay leaf to the pot for additional flavor.

Simmer:
- Bring the mixture to a boil, then reduce the heat to low. Cover the pot and simmer for 1.5 to 2 hours, or until the beans are tender. Stir occasionally and add more water if needed.

Adjust Seasoning:
- Taste the Charro Beans and adjust the seasoning with salt and pepper as needed.

Serve:
- Remove the bay leaf and serve the Charro Beans hot. Optionally, serve with fresh lime wedges on the side for squeezing over the beans.

Enjoy your homemade Charro Beans as a flavorful and satisfying side dish or as a main course with rice or tortillas! The combination of bacon, tomatoes, and seasonings gives these beans a rich and savory taste.

Mexican Street Corn Salad (Esquites) Recipe

Ingredients:

For the Salad:

- 4 cups corn kernels (fresh or frozen)
- 2 tablespoons vegetable oil
- 1/2 cup mayonnaise
- 1/2 cup crumbled cotija cheese (or feta cheese)
- 1/4 cup finely chopped fresh cilantro
- 1 jalapeño, finely chopped (seeds removed for less heat)
- 1 clove garlic, minced
- Juice of 1 lime
- Salt and pepper to taste

For Garnish:

- Additional crumbled cotija cheese
- Chili powder or paprika
- Lime wedges

Instructions:

Cook Corn:
- If using fresh corn, remove kernels from the cobs. If using frozen corn, thaw it. In a large skillet, heat vegetable oil over medium heat. Add the corn kernels and cook until they are golden brown and slightly charred.

Make the Dressing:
- In a small bowl, mix together mayonnaise, crumbled cotija cheese, chopped cilantro, chopped jalapeño, minced garlic, lime juice, salt, and pepper.

Combine Corn and Dressing:
- Transfer the cooked corn to a large bowl. Pour the dressing over the corn and toss to coat evenly.

Chill (Optional):
- If time allows, refrigerate the Mexican Street Corn Salad for about 30 minutes to let the flavors meld.

Garnish and Serve:

- Before serving, garnish the salad with additional crumbled cotija cheese, a sprinkle of chili powder or paprika, and lime wedges on the side.

Enjoy your homemade Mexican Street Corn Salad as a delicious and festive side dish or as a topping for tacos, grilled meats, or nachos! The combination of charred corn, creamy dressing, and flavorful toppings creates a dish that's both refreshing and satisfying.

Chayote Squash Salad Recipe

Ingredients:

For the Salad:

- 2 chayote squash, peeled and julienned
- 1 cucumber, thinly sliced
- 1 red bell pepper, thinly sliced
- 1/2 red onion, thinly sliced
- 1/4 cup fresh cilantro, chopped
- 1 avocado, diced
- 1/4 cup crumbled queso fresco or feta cheese (optional)

For the Dressing:

- Juice of 2 limes
- 2 tablespoons olive oil
- 1 clove garlic, minced
- 1 teaspoon honey or agave nectar
- Salt and pepper to taste

Instructions:

Prepare the Salad:

Prepare Chayote Squash:
- Peel the chayote squash and julienne it into thin strips. You can use a mandoline or a julienne peeler for this.

Combine Ingredients:
- In a large salad bowl, combine the julienned chayote squash, sliced cucumber, sliced red bell pepper, thinly sliced red onion, chopped cilantro, and diced avocado.

Prepare the Dressing:

Whisk the Dressing:
- In a small bowl, whisk together the lime juice, olive oil, minced garlic, honey or agave nectar, salt, and pepper.

Dress the Salad:

- Pour the dressing over the salad ingredients. Toss gently to coat the vegetables evenly with the dressing.

Add Cheese (Optional):
- If using, sprinkle crumbled queso fresco or feta cheese over the salad.

Serve:

Serve the Chayote Squash Salad immediately as a refreshing side dish or light lunch option!

Note: Chayote squash can be eaten raw, and its mild flavor makes it a great addition to salads. This salad is not only tasty but also offers a wonderful combination of textures and colors.

Feel free to customize the salad with additional ingredients such as cherry tomatoes, black beans, or grilled chicken, depending on your preferences. Enjoy this Chayote Squash Salad for a healthy and vibrant meal!

Salsa Fresca (Pico de Gallo) Recipe

Ingredients:

- 4 medium-sized tomatoes, diced
- 1/2 red onion, finely chopped
- 1 jalapeño, seeds removed and finely chopped
- 1/4 cup fresh cilantro, chopped
- Juice of 1-2 limes
- Salt and pepper to taste

Instructions:

Prepare the Ingredients:
- Dice the tomatoes, finely chop the red onion, remove the seeds from the jalapeño and finely chop it, and chop the fresh cilantro.

Combine Ingredients:
- In a mixing bowl, combine the diced tomatoes, chopped red onion, chopped jalapeño, and chopped cilantro.

Add Lime Juice:
- Squeeze the juice of one or two limes over the mixture, depending on your taste preference.

Season:
- Season the Salsa Fresca with salt and pepper to taste. Stir well to combine.

Chill (Optional):
- If time allows, refrigerate the salsa for about 30 minutes to let the flavors meld.

Adjust Seasoning:
- Taste the salsa and adjust the lime juice, salt, and pepper to your liking.

Serve:
- Serve Salsa Fresca immediately as a topping for tacos, grilled meats, nachos, or as a dip with tortilla chips.

Enjoy your homemade Salsa Fresca as a fresh and zesty addition to your favorite Mexican dishes! This simple and colorful salsa brings a burst of flavor and freshness to any meal.

Sauces and Condiments:

Red Enchilada Sauce Recipe

Ingredients:

- 2 tablespoons vegetable oil
- 2 tablespoons all-purpose flour
- 3 tablespoons chili powder
- 1 teaspoon ground cumin
- 1/2 teaspoon garlic powder
- 1/4 teaspoon onion powder
- 1/4 teaspoon dried oregano
- 2 cups chicken or vegetable broth
- 1 can (14 ounces) crushed tomatoes
- Salt and pepper to taste

Instructions:

Prepare the Roux:
- In a medium-sized saucepan, heat the vegetable oil over medium heat. Add the flour and whisk continuously to create a roux. Cook for 1-2 minutes until the roux becomes lightly golden.

Add Spices:
- Stir in the chili powder, ground cumin, garlic powder, onion powder, and dried oregano. Cook for an additional 1-2 minutes to toast the spices.

Gradually Add Liquid:
- Gradually whisk in the chicken or vegetable broth to avoid lumps. Continue whisking until the mixture is smooth.

Incorporate Crushed Tomatoes:
- Add the crushed tomatoes to the saucepan. Stir well to combine.

Simmer:
- Bring the sauce to a simmer over medium heat. Reduce the heat to low and let it simmer for 15-20 minutes, stirring occasionally.

Season:
- Season the red enchilada sauce with salt and pepper to taste. Adjust the seasoning as needed.

Blend (Optional):

- If you prefer a smoother consistency, you can use an immersion blender to blend the sauce until smooth. Be cautious as the sauce will be hot.

Use or Store:
- Once the sauce reaches your desired consistency and flavor, it's ready to use. You can use it immediately for enchiladas or store it in a sealed container in the refrigerator for later use.

Enjoy your homemade Red Enchilada Sauce as a flavorful base for enchiladas, tamales, or any Mexican-inspired dishes! Adjust the level of spiciness by modifying the amount of chili powder, and feel free to customize the flavors to suit your taste.

Tomatillo Salsa (Salsa Verde) Recipe

Ingredients:

- 1 pound tomatillos, husked and rinsed
- 2-3 serrano or jalapeño peppers (adjust to taste)
- 1/2 onion, roughly chopped
- 2 cloves garlic, peeled
- 1/2 cup fresh cilantro, chopped
- Juice of 1-2 limes
- Salt to taste

Instructions:

Prepare Tomatillos:
- Remove the husks from the tomatillos and rinse them under cold water to remove the sticky residue.

Roast Tomatillos and Peppers:
- Preheat the broiler in your oven. Place the tomatillos and chili peppers on a baking sheet. Broil for 5-7 minutes, turning them halfway, until they are charred and softened.

Blend Ingredients:
- In a blender or food processor, combine the roasted tomatillos, roasted chili peppers, chopped onion, peeled garlic cloves, and cilantro.

Add Lime Juice and Salt:
- Squeeze the juice of 1-2 limes into the blender, depending on your taste preference. Add salt to taste.

Blend Until Smooth:
- Blend the ingredients until you achieve a smooth consistency. If you prefer a chunkier salsa, pulse the ingredients to your desired texture.

Adjust Seasoning:
- Taste the tomatillo salsa and adjust the lime juice and salt if needed.

Chill (Optional):
- Refrigerate the salsa for at least 30 minutes before serving to allow the flavors to meld. This step is optional but can enhance the overall taste.

Serve:
- Serve Tomatillo Salsa as a condiment for tacos, enchiladas, grilled meats, or as a dip with tortilla chips.

Enjoy your homemade Tomatillo Salsa (Salsa Verde) with its tangy and slightly spicy flavor! This versatile salsa adds a burst of freshness and zest to a variety of dishes. Adjust the level of spiciness by adding or reducing the number of chili peppers.

Chipotle Adobo Sauce Recipe

Ingredients:

- 6-8 dried chipotle peppers
- 2 cups hot water (for soaking)
- 3 cloves garlic, minced
- 1/2 cup tomato puree or crushed tomatoes
- 1/4 cup apple cider vinegar
- 1 tablespoon olive oil
- 1 teaspoon dried oregano
- 1 teaspoon ground cumin
- 1/2 teaspoon smoked paprika
- Salt to taste

Instructions:

Soak Chipotle Peppers:
- Place the dried chipotle peppers in a bowl and cover them with hot water. Let them soak for 20-30 minutes until they become pliable.

Prepare the Peppers:
- Once the chipotle peppers are rehydrated, remove the stems and seeds. You can wear gloves to protect your hands from the heat.

Blend Ingredients:
- In a blender or food processor, combine the soaked chipotle peppers, minced garlic, tomato puree or crushed tomatoes, apple cider vinegar, olive oil, dried oregano, ground cumin, smoked paprika, and salt.

Blend Until Smooth:
- Blend the ingredients until you achieve a smooth and thick consistency. If the sauce is too thick, you can add a little water to reach your desired texture.

Strain (Optional):
- If you prefer a smoother sauce, you can strain it using a fine mesh sieve to remove any remaining bits of pepper skin or seeds.

Cook:
- In a saucepan, heat the chipotle adobo sauce over medium heat. Simmer for 10-15 minutes to allow the flavors to meld and the sauce to thicken.

Adjust Seasoning:
- Taste the sauce and adjust the seasoning if needed. You can add more salt, vinegar, or spices to suit your taste.

Cool and Store:
- Allow the Chipotle Adobo Sauce to cool before storing it in a jar or airtight container in the refrigerator. It can be stored for several weeks.

Use your homemade Chipotle Adobo Sauce as a versatile and smoky condiment for marinades, dressings, or as a flavor enhancer for various dishes! Adjust the level of heat by controlling the number of chipotle peppers used in the recipe.

Pico de Gallo Recipe

Ingredients:

- 4 medium-sized tomatoes, diced
- 1/2 red onion, finely chopped
- 1-2 jalapeño peppers, seeds removed and finely chopped
- 1/4 cup fresh cilantro, chopped
- Juice of 1-2 limes
- Salt to taste

Instructions:

Prepare the Ingredients:
- Dice the tomatoes, finely chop the red onion, remove the seeds from the jalapeño peppers, and finely chop them. Chop the fresh cilantro.

Combine Ingredients:
- In a mixing bowl, combine the diced tomatoes, chopped red onion, chopped jalapeños, and chopped cilantro.

Add Lime Juice:
- Squeeze the juice of 1-2 limes into the bowl, depending on your taste preference.

Season:
- Sprinkle salt over the mixture to taste.

Mix Well:
- Gently toss the ingredients together until well combined. Be careful not to mash the tomatoes.

Chill (Optional):
- If time allows, refrigerate the Pico de Gallo for about 30 minutes before serving to let the flavors meld.

Adjust Seasoning:
- Taste the Pico de Gallo and adjust the lime juice and salt if needed.

Serve:
- Serve Pico de Gallo immediately as a topping for tacos, grilled meats, nachos, or as a dip with tortilla chips.

Enjoy your homemade Pico de Gallo as a fresh and zesty accompaniment to your favorite Mexican dishes! This simple salsa is known for its vibrant colors and flavors, making it a perfect addition to many meals. Adjust the level of spiciness by modifying the amount of jalapeños used in the recipe.

Habanero Hot Sauce Recipe

Ingredients:

- 10-12 habanero peppers, stems removed
- 3 cloves garlic, minced
- 1 medium carrot, peeled and chopped
- 1/2 onion, chopped
- 1 cup white vinegar
- 1 cup water
- 1 tablespoon olive oil
- 1 teaspoon salt
- 1/2 teaspoon sugar (optional, to balance the heat)
- Gloves (recommended when handling habanero peppers)

Instructions:

Prepare Ingredients:
- Wear gloves to protect your hands from the heat of the habanero peppers. Remove the stems from the habaneros and roughly chop them. Peel and chop the carrot, chop the onion, and mince the garlic.

Sauté Vegetables:
- In a saucepan, heat the olive oil over medium heat. Add the chopped habanero peppers, minced garlic, chopped carrot, and chopped onion. Sauté for about 5-7 minutes until the vegetables are softened.

Add Liquid Ingredients:
- Pour in the white vinegar and water. Allow the mixture to come to a simmer.

Simmer:
- Simmer the mixture over low heat for 15-20 minutes until the vegetables are tender.

Blend:
- Using an immersion blender or a regular blender, carefully blend the mixture until smooth. Be cautious when blending hot liquids, and allow the mixture to cool slightly if needed.

Strain (Optional):
- If you prefer a smoother hot sauce, you can strain the blended mixture using a fine mesh sieve to remove any solids.

Season:

- Add salt and sugar (optional) to the blended mixture. Adjust the seasoning to your taste.

Cool and Store:
- Allow the Habanero Hot Sauce to cool completely before transferring it to a bottle or jar. Store it in the refrigerator.

Enjoy your homemade Habanero Hot Sauce as a spicy condiment for tacos, grilled meats, or any dish that needs a fiery kick! Adjust the number of habanero peppers to control the heat level, and feel free to experiment with additional spices for flavor variation.

Salsa Ranchera Recipe

Ingredients:

- 4 medium-sized tomatoes, diced
- 1/2 onion, finely chopped
- 2 jalapeño peppers, seeds removed and finely chopped
- 2 cloves garlic, minced
- 1 tablespoon vegetable oil
- 1 teaspoon dried oregano
- 1 teaspoon ground cumin
- 1/2 teaspoon smoked paprika
- Salt and pepper to taste
- 1 cup tomato sauce or crushed tomatoes
- 1/2 cup chicken or vegetable broth (optional, for a thinner consistency)

Instructions:

Prepare Ingredients:
- Dice the tomatoes, finely chop the onion, remove the seeds from the jalapeño peppers and finely chop them, and mince the garlic.

Sauté Aromatics:
- In a saucepan, heat the vegetable oil over medium heat. Add the chopped onion and jalapeños. Sauté until the onion is translucent.

Add Tomatoes and Garlic:
- Add the diced tomatoes and minced garlic to the saucepan. Cook for a few minutes until the tomatoes start to soften.

Season:
- Sprinkle dried oregano, ground cumin, smoked paprika, salt, and pepper over the tomato mixture. Stir to combine.

Incorporate Tomato Sauce:
- Pour in the tomato sauce or crushed tomatoes. If you prefer a thinner consistency, add chicken or vegetable broth.

Simmer:
- Bring the mixture to a simmer, then reduce the heat to low. Allow it to simmer for 15-20 minutes, stirring occasionally, until the flavors meld and the sauce thickens.

Adjust Seasoning:
- Taste the Salsa Ranchera and adjust the seasoning with additional salt or spices if needed.

Serve:
- Serve Salsa Ranchera as a condiment for eggs, tacos, grilled meats, or any dish that could use a flavorful kick.

Enjoy your homemade Salsa Ranchera with its rich and savory flavor! This versatile sauce can be customized to your taste preferences by adjusting the level of spiciness or experimenting with additional spices.

Roasted Garlic Guacamole Recipe

Ingredients:

- 3 ripe avocados
- 1 head of garlic
- 1 tablespoon olive oil
- Juice of 1 lime
- 1/2 red onion, finely diced
- 1-2 jalapeño peppers, seeds removed and finely chopped
- 1/4 cup fresh cilantro, chopped
- Salt and pepper to taste
- Optional: cherry tomatoes, diced, for garnish

Instructions:

Roast the Garlic:
- Preheat the oven to 400°F (200°C). Cut the top off the head of garlic to expose the cloves. Place the garlic head on a piece of foil, drizzle it with olive oil, and wrap it in the foil. Roast in the oven for about 30-40 minutes or until the garlic cloves are soft and golden brown. Allow it to cool.

Prepare Avocados:
- Cut the avocados in half, remove the pits, and scoop the flesh into a mixing bowl.

Mash Avocados:
- Use a fork or potato masher to mash the avocados to your desired consistency.

Squeeze Roasted Garlic:
- Squeeze the roasted garlic cloves out of their skins. Mash them with a fork and add them to the mashed avocados.

Add Lime Juice:
- Squeeze the juice of one lime over the avocados and roasted garlic. Mix well to combine.

Incorporate Vegetables:
- Add finely diced red onion, chopped jalapeños, and fresh cilantro to the mixture. If you like, you can also add diced cherry tomatoes for extra freshness.

Season:
- Season the guacamole with salt and pepper to taste. Adjust the seasoning as needed.

Serve:
- Serve the Roasted Garlic Guacamole immediately with tortilla chips, as a topping for tacos, or alongside your favorite dishes.

Enjoy your homemade Roasted Garlic Guacamole with its enhanced flavor from the roasted garlic! The roasted garlic adds a sweet and savory dimension to the creamy avocados, creating a delicious and memorable guacamole.

Pickled Red Onions Recipe

Ingredients:

- 1 medium-sized red onion, thinly sliced
- 3/4 cup apple cider vinegar
- 1 tablespoon sugar
- 1 1/2 teaspoons salt
- 1 cup warm water
- Optional: 1-2 cloves of garlic, smashed
- Optional: 1 teaspoon whole black peppercorns
- Optional: 1 bay leaf

Instructions:

Prepare the Red Onions:
- Peel the red onion and thinly slice it into rings or half-moons. Place the sliced onions in a clean and heatproof jar or bowl.

Prepare the Pickling Liquid:
- In a separate bowl, combine apple cider vinegar, sugar, and salt. Stir until the sugar and salt are dissolved.

Add Optional Ingredients:
- If desired, add smashed garlic cloves, whole black peppercorns, and a bay leaf to the pickling liquid. These optional ingredients can add additional flavor to the pickled onions.

Pour Pickling Liquid:
- Pour the pickling liquid over the sliced red onions. Make sure the onions are fully submerged in the liquid.

Add Warm Water:
- Pour warm water over the onions and pickling liquid to cover them completely.

Stir and Let Sit:
- Gently stir the mixture to combine. Allow the pickled red onions to sit at room temperature for about 1 hour. This helps the flavors meld.

Refrigerate:
- After an hour, cover the jar or bowl and refrigerate the pickled red onions for at least 2-3 hours, or overnight for the best flavor.

Serve:

- Once chilled and pickled to your liking, the pickled red onions are ready to use. They can be served as a topping for tacos, salads, sandwiches, burgers, or any dish that could use a burst of tangy flavor.

Enjoy your homemade Pickled Red Onions as a delicious and vibrant condiment! These pickled onions can be stored in the refrigerator for up to a few weeks. Adjust the sweetness and acidity levels to your taste preference by modifying the sugar and vinegar amounts.

Ancho Chili Paste Recipe

Ingredients:

- 6-8 dried ancho chili peppers
- 2 cloves garlic, minced
- 1 teaspoon ground cumin
- 1 teaspoon dried oregano
- 1/2 teaspoon salt
- 1/4 cup olive oil
- 1 tablespoon apple cider vinegar

Instructions:

Prepare Ancho Chilies:
- Remove the stems and seeds from the dried ancho chili peppers. You can do this by cutting them open and shaking out the seeds.

Rehydrate Chilies:
- Place the ancho chili peppers in a bowl and cover them with hot water. Let them soak for about 20-30 minutes until they become soft and pliable.

Make the Ancho Paste:
- In a blender or food processor, combine the rehydrated ancho chili peppers, minced garlic, ground cumin, dried oregano, salt, olive oil, and apple cider vinegar.

Blend Until Smooth:
- Blend the ingredients until you achieve a smooth paste-like consistency. You may need to scrape down the sides of the blender or food processor to ensure everything is well incorporated.

Adjust Consistency:
- If the paste is too thick, you can add a bit more olive oil or water and blend again until you reach your desired consistency.

Taste and Adjust:
- Taste the Ancho Chili Paste and adjust the seasoning as needed. You can add more salt, cumin, or vinegar based on your preference.

Store:
- Transfer the Ancho Chili Paste to a jar or airtight container. It can be stored in the refrigerator for several weeks.

Enjoy your homemade Ancho Chili Paste as a versatile and flavorful addition to various dishes! This paste can be used to add depth and smokiness to soups, stews, marinades, sauces, or as a rub for meats. Adjust the spiciness by controlling the number of ancho peppers and seeds used in the recipe.

Mango Habanero Salsa Recipe

Ingredients:

- 2 ripe mangoes, peeled, pitted, and diced
- 1-2 habanero peppers, seeds and membranes removed, finely chopped
- 1/2 red onion, finely diced
- 1/4 cup fresh cilantro, chopped
- Juice of 2 limes
- Salt to taste
- Optional: 1 red bell pepper, diced, for extra color
- Optional: 1 tablespoon honey or agave nectar for added sweetness

Instructions:

Prepare Ingredients:
- Peel, pit, and dice the ripe mangoes. Finely chop the habanero peppers after removing the seeds and membranes. Finely dice the red onion, and chop the fresh cilantro.

Combine Ingredients:
- In a mixing bowl, combine the diced mangoes, chopped habanero peppers, diced red onion, and chopped cilantro. If you like, add diced red bell pepper for additional color.

Add Lime Juice:
- Squeeze the juice of two limes over the mango mixture. The acidity of the lime juice will enhance the flavors.

Optional Sweetener:
- If you prefer a sweeter salsa, you can add honey or agave nectar to taste. Start with 1 tablespoon and adjust as needed.

Season with Salt:
- Sprinkle salt over the salsa to taste. Start with a small amount and adjust as necessary.

Mix Well:
- Gently toss the ingredients together until well combined. Be careful not to mash the mango pieces.

Chill (Optional):
- Refrigerate the Mango Habanero Salsa for about 30 minutes to allow the flavors to meld. This step is optional but can enhance the overall taste.

Serve:

- Serve the salsa as a refreshing topping for grilled chicken, fish, tacos, or as a dip with tortilla chips.

Enjoy your homemade Mango Habanero Salsa with its sweet, spicy, and tropical flavors! This salsa is a fantastic accompaniment to various dishes and is sure to add a burst of flavor to your meals. Adjust the level of spiciness by modifying the number of habanero peppers used in the recipe.

Breakfast and Brunch:

Chilaquiles Recipe

Ingredients:

- 6 cups tortilla chips (store-bought or homemade)
- 1 1/2 cups red or green salsa (homemade or store-bought)
- 1 cup shredded cooked chicken (optional)
- 1/2 cup diced red onion
- 1/2 cup crumbled queso fresco or feta cheese
- 1/4 cup chopped fresh cilantro
- 2 tablespoons sour cream (optional)
- 2 fried or poached eggs (optional)
- Salt and pepper to taste
- Vegetable oil for frying (if making your own tortilla chips)

Instructions:

Prepare Tortilla Chips:
- If not using store-bought chips, cut corn tortillas into strips or triangles. Heat vegetable oil in a pan and fry the tortilla pieces until golden and crispy. Drain on paper towels.

Make the Salsa:
- If you don't have store-bought salsa, prepare your preferred red or green salsa. You can use a blender to blend tomatoes, chili peppers, garlic, and other seasonings for a homemade version.

Assemble Chilaquiles:
- In a large skillet, heat the salsa over medium heat. Once it simmers, add the tortilla chips to the skillet, tossing them until they are evenly coated with the salsa.

Add Chicken (Optional):
- If using shredded chicken, add it to the skillet, tossing to combine with the chips and salsa. Allow the mixture to cook for a few minutes until everything is heated through.

Serve:
- Transfer the chilaquiles to a serving platter. Top with diced red onion, crumbled queso fresco or feta cheese, and chopped fresh cilantro.

Optional Toppings:

- Optionally, add a dollop of sour cream and place fried or poached eggs on top of the chilaquiles.

Season:
- Season the chilaquiles with salt and pepper to taste.

Serve Immediately:
- Chilaquiles are best served immediately while the tortilla chips are still crispy.

Enjoy your easy and delicious Chilaquiles! Feel free to customize with your favorite toppings and make it your own.

Huevos Rancheros Recipe

Ingredients:

- 4 corn tortillas
- 4 large eggs
- 1 cup black beans, cooked and mashed (optional)
- 1 cup shredded Mexican cheese blend
- 1 cup salsa (homemade or store-bought)
- 1/2 cup diced tomatoes
- 1/4 cup chopped fresh cilantro
- 1/4 cup diced red onion
- 1-2 tablespoons vegetable oil
- Salt and pepper to taste
- Avocado slices for garnish (optional)
- Lime wedges for serving

Instructions:

Prepare Tortillas:
- Heat the tortillas in a dry skillet or directly over a gas flame until they are warm and slightly toasted. Keep them warm by wrapping in a clean kitchen towel.

Cook Eggs:
- In the same skillet, add vegetable oil over medium heat. Crack the eggs into the skillet and cook them to your desired doneness. Season with salt and pepper.

Warm Black Beans (Optional):
- If using black beans, warm them in a small saucepan or in the microwave. Mash them slightly with a fork.

Assemble Huevos Rancheros:
- Place a warm tortilla on a plate. Spread a layer of mashed black beans if using. Top with a fried egg.

Add Sauce and Cheese:
- Spoon salsa over the egg and sprinkle shredded cheese on top.

Garnish:
- Garnish with diced tomatoes, chopped cilantro, and diced red onion. Add avocado slices if desired.

Repeat:
- Repeat the process for the remaining tortillas and eggs.

Serve:
- Serve the Huevos Rancheros immediately, accompanied by lime wedges on the side.

Enjoy your delicious Huevos Rancheros for a hearty and satisfying breakfast! This dish is customizable, so feel free to adjust the toppings and spice level according to your preferences.

Breakfast Burritos Recipe

Ingredients:

- 4 large flour tortillas
- 6 large eggs
- 1/4 cup milk
- Salt and pepper to taste
- 1 tablespoon butter or oil for cooking
- 1 cup cooked and diced breakfast potatoes (hash browns or diced cooked potatoes)
- 1 cup cooked and crumbled breakfast sausage or bacon
- 1 cup shredded cheese (cheddar, Monterey Jack, or your favorite blend)
- 1/2 cup salsa
- Optional toppings: diced tomatoes, sliced avocado, chopped cilantro, sour cream

Instructions:

Prepare Ingredients:
- Cook breakfast potatoes and set aside. Cook and crumble the breakfast sausage or bacon. Shred the cheese and prepare any additional toppings.

Scramble Eggs:
- In a bowl, whisk together eggs, milk, salt, and pepper. Heat butter or oil in a skillet over medium heat. Pour the egg mixture into the skillet and scramble until cooked to your liking.

Assemble Burritos:
- Warm the flour tortillas in a dry skillet or in the microwave. Place a portion of the scrambled eggs, cooked potatoes, and crumbled sausage or bacon in the center of each tortilla.

Add Cheese and Salsa:
- Sprinkle shredded cheese over the fillings, and spoon salsa on top.

Fold and Roll:
- Fold the sides of the tortilla over the filling and then roll it up tightly, forming a burrito.

Optional: Toast or Grill (Optional):
- For added flavor, you can toast the assembled burritos on a hot skillet or grill for a few minutes until they have a golden-brown color.

Serve:
- Serve the breakfast burritos immediately with optional toppings such as diced tomatoes, sliced avocado, chopped cilantro, and sour cream.

Enjoy your homemade Breakfast Burritos for a satisfying and portable morning meal! These burritos are versatile, so feel free to customize them with your favorite ingredients and toppings.

Machaca (Shredded Beef and Eggs) Recipe

Ingredients:

- 1 pound flank steak or beef roast
- 1 onion, finely chopped
- 2 tomatoes, diced
- 3 cloves garlic, minced
- 1 jalapeño, seeds removed and finely chopped
- 1 bell pepper, diced
- 4 large eggs
- 1/4 cup chopped fresh cilantro
- 2 tablespoons vegetable oil
- Salt and pepper to taste
- Flour tortillas for serving
- Optional toppings: salsa, sliced avocado, shredded cheese

Instructions:

Prepare the Beef:
- Season the flank steak or beef roast with salt and pepper. In a large skillet or slow cooker, cook the beef until tender and easily shredded. This can be done by simmering on the stovetop or slow cooking until the beef is easily pulled apart with a fork. Once cooked, shred the beef.

Sauté Vegetables:
- In a separate skillet, heat vegetable oil over medium heat. Add chopped onion, diced tomatoes, minced garlic, chopped jalapeño, and diced bell pepper. Sauté until the vegetables are softened.

Combine Beef and Vegetables:
- Add the shredded beef to the sautéed vegetables. Mix well and continue cooking for a few minutes to allow the flavors to meld.

Add Eggs:
- Make a well in the center of the beef and vegetable mixture. Crack the eggs into the well. Allow them to cook slightly before stirring to scramble and combine with the beef.

Finish Cooking:
- Continue cooking until the eggs are fully cooked and mixed with the beef and vegetables. Add chopped cilantro and adjust the seasoning with salt and pepper.

Serve:

- Spoon the Machaca mixture onto warm flour tortillas. Serve with optional toppings such as salsa, sliced avocado, and shredded cheese.

Enjoy your homemade Machaca, a delicious and hearty dish perfect for breakfast or brunch! Adjust the level of spiciness by controlling the amount of jalapeño used or by adding hot sauce to taste.

Sopes with Eggs and Chorizo Recipe

Ingredients:

For the Sopes:

- 2 cups masa harina (corn masa flour)
- 1 1/4 cups warm water
- 1/2 teaspoon salt
- Vegetable oil for frying

For the Toppings:

- 1/2 pound chorizo, removed from casings
- 4 large eggs
- 1 cup refried beans
- 1 cup shredded lettuce
- 1 cup diced tomatoes
- 1/2 cup crumbled queso fresco or feta cheese
- 1/4 cup chopped fresh cilantro
- 1/4 cup diced red onion
- Lime wedges for serving

Instructions:

For the Sopes:

   Prepare the Masa Dough:
   - In a large bowl, mix masa harina, warm water, and salt until a soft, pliable dough forms.

   Form the Sopes:
   - Take a golf ball-sized portion of the dough and roll it into a ball. Flatten it into a thick disk (about 1/4 inch thick) with raised edges to form the sope. Repeat for the remaining dough.

   Cook the Sopes:
   - Heat vegetable oil in a skillet over medium heat. Fry the sopes on both sides until golden brown. Drain on paper towels.

For the Toppings:

Cook Chorizo:
- In a separate skillet, cook the chorizo over medium heat, breaking it apart with a spatula as it cooks. Once cooked through, set aside.

Scramble Eggs:
- In the same skillet, scramble the eggs until just cooked. Mix the cooked chorizo with the scrambled eggs.

Assemble the Sopes:
- Spread a layer of refried beans onto each sope. Top with the chorizo and egg mixture.

Add Fresh Toppings:
- Garnish the sopes with shredded lettuce, diced tomatoes, crumbled queso fresco, chopped cilantro, and diced red onion.

Serve:
- Serve the Sopes with Eggs and Chorizo immediately, accompanied by lime wedges for squeezing over the top.

Enjoy your delicious Sopes with Eggs and Chorizo, a flavorful and hearty Mexican dish! Customize the toppings to your liking and add a drizzle of hot sauce if you enjoy extra spice.

Mexican French Toast (Capirotada) Recipe

Ingredients:

- 8 slices of bolillo or French bread, slightly stale
- 1 cup shredded Monterey Jack cheese
- 1 cup raisins or currants
- 1 cup chopped walnuts or pecans
- 1 cup grated coconut (optional)
- 2 cinnamon sticks
- 4 cups water
- 2 cups dark brown sugar
- 1 cup unsalted butter
- Ground cinnamon for dusting

Instructions:

Prepare the Bread:
- Cut the bread into cubes or slices.

Prepare the Syrup:
- In a saucepan, combine water, dark brown sugar, and cinnamon sticks. Bring to a boil, then reduce heat and simmer for 10-15 minutes to create a flavorful syrup. Remove the cinnamon sticks.

Assemble the Capirotada:
- In a greased baking dish, layer half of the bread cubes. Sprinkle half of the shredded cheese, raisins, chopped nuts, and grated coconut (if using) over the bread. Repeat with another layer using the remaining ingredients.

Pour the Syrup:
- Pour the warm syrup over the layered bread and ingredients, ensuring that the bread is well-soaked.

Add Butter:
- Cut the unsalted butter into small pieces and scatter them over the top of the capirotada.

Bake:
- Cover the baking dish with aluminum foil and bake in a preheated oven at 350°F (175°C) for approximately 30-40 minutes or until the bread is soft and the top is golden brown.

Cool:
- Allow the Capirotada to cool for a few minutes before serving.

Serve:

- Serve the Mexican French Toast warm, dusted with ground cinnamon. It can be enjoyed as a dessert or a sweet breakfast dish.

Enjoy your homemade Mexican French Toast (Capirotada)! This unique and flavorful bread pudding is a delightful treat with its combination of sweet and savory elements.

Molletes Recipe

Ingredients:

- 4 bolillo rolls or telera rolls, split in half
- 2 cups refried beans (homemade or canned)
- 2 cups shredded Oaxaca cheese or Monterey Jack cheese
- 1/2 cup pico de gallo or salsa
- Pickled jalapeño slices (optional)
- Fresh cilantro, chopped, for garnish
- Salt and pepper to taste

Instructions:

Preheat the Oven:
- Preheat your oven to a broil setting.

Prepare the Bread:
- Cut the bolillo or telera rolls in half horizontally. Place the halves on a baking sheet.

Toast the Bread:
- Toast the bread under the broiler for a few minutes until it becomes lightly golden. Keep a close eye to prevent burning.

Spread Refried Beans:
- Spread a generous layer of refried beans onto each toasted bread half.

Add Cheese:
- Sprinkle a generous amount of shredded cheese over the refried beans on each bread half.

Broil Until Cheese Melts:
- Place the baking sheet back under the broiler and broil until the cheese is melted and bubbly, and the edges of the bread are golden brown.

Top with Salsa and Jalapeños:
- Remove the molletes from the oven and top each with a spoonful of pico de gallo or salsa. Add pickled jalapeño slices if desired.

Garnish and Season:
- Garnish the molletes with chopped fresh cilantro. Add salt and pepper to taste.

Serve Immediately:
- Molletes are best enjoyed warm. Serve them immediately as a delicious and satisfying breakfast or snack.

Enjoy your homemade Molletes! Feel free to customize them with additional toppings like avocado slices, sour cream, or crumbled queso fresco based on your preferences.

Nopalitos Omelette Recipe

Ingredients:

- 4 large eggs
- 1/2 cup nopalitos (prickly pear cactus paddles), cleaned and diced
- 1/4 cup diced onion
- 1/4 cup diced tomatoes
- 1/4 cup diced bell peppers (any color)
- 1/4 cup shredded cheese (cheddar, Monterey Jack, or your choice)
- 1 tablespoon chopped fresh cilantro
- Salt and pepper to taste
- 1 tablespoon olive oil or butter for cooking
- Optional toppings: salsa, avocado slices, sour cream

Instructions:

Prepare Nopalitos:
- Clean the nopalitos by removing the thorns and spines. Dice them into small pieces.

Sauté Vegetables:
- In a skillet, heat olive oil or butter over medium heat. Add diced onion, nopalitos, tomatoes, and bell peppers. Sauté until the vegetables are tender.

Whisk Eggs:
- In a bowl, whisk the eggs until well beaten. Season with salt and pepper.

Add Eggs to Vegetables:
- Pour the beaten eggs over the sautéed vegetables in the skillet. Allow the eggs to set slightly around the edges.

Add Cheese and Cilantro:
- Sprinkle shredded cheese and chopped cilantro over one half of the omelette.

Fold and Cook:
- Gently fold the other half of the omelette over the cheese and cilantro. Cook until the eggs are fully set and the cheese is melted.

Serve:
- Slide the Nopalitos Omelette onto a plate. Garnish with additional cilantro and serve with optional toppings such as salsa, avocado slices, or sour cream.

Enjoy:

- Enjoy your Nopalitos Omelette as a flavorful and nutritious breakfast or brunch.

Note: Nopalitos have a mild, slightly tangy flavor and are known for their health benefits. Make sure to clean them thoroughly and remove any thorns before cooking.

Feel free to customize this recipe by adding other ingredients like diced jalapeños, black beans, or crumbled queso fresco.

Sweet Tamales (Tamales de Dulce) Recipe

Ingredients:

For the Masa:

- 2 cups masa harina (corn masa flour)
- 1 cup unsalted butter, softened
- 1 cup granulated sugar
- 1 teaspoon baking powder
- 1/2 teaspoon salt
- 1 cup warm milk or water (approximately)

For the Filling:

- 1 cup sweetened shredded coconut
- 1 cup raisins or dried fruit (e.g., chopped apricots, figs)
- 1 cup chopped nuts (e.g., almonds, pecans)
- 1 teaspoon ground cinnamon
- 1/2 cup honey or agave syrup

Corn Husks:

- Dried corn husks, soaked in warm water for at least 30 minutes

Instructions:

Prepare the Corn Husks:
- Soak the dried corn husks in warm water for at least 30 minutes or until they are pliable.

Make the Masa:
- In a large mixing bowl, beat the softened butter until creamy. Add the sugar and continue beating until well combined.
- In a separate bowl, mix the masa harina, baking powder, and salt.
- Gradually add the masa harina mixture to the butter and sugar, alternating with warm milk or water, until a smooth and spreadable consistency is achieved.

Prepare the Filling:
- In a separate bowl, combine sweetened shredded coconut, raisins or dried fruit, chopped nuts, ground cinnamon, and honey or agave syrup. Mix well.

Assemble the Tamales:
- Take a soaked corn husk and spread a thin layer of the masa mixture over the center, leaving space around the edges.

- Spoon a generous tablespoon of the sweet filling along the center of the masa.

Fold and Tie:
- Fold the sides of the corn husk over the filling, then fold the top and bottom to enclose the tamale. Tie with strips of soaked corn husk or kitchen twine.

Steam the Tamales:
- Arrange the tamales upright in a steamer basket. Steam over boiling water for approximately 1 to 1.5 hours, or until the masa is firm.

Serve:
- Allow the tamales to cool for a few minutes before serving. Serve warm and enjoy your Sweet Tamales!

Note: You can get creative with the fillings by adding ingredients like chocolate chips, fruit preserves, or other sweet additions. The steaming time may vary, so check for doneness by ensuring the masa is cooked through and has a firm texture.

Mexican Hot Chocolate Recipe

Ingredients:

- 4 cups whole milk
- 3 ounces Mexican chocolate (tablet or disks), chopped
- 2 tablespoons cocoa powder
- 1/4 cup granulated sugar (adjust to taste)
- 1 cinnamon stick
- 1/4 teaspoon ground cinnamon (optional, for extra flavor)
- 1/4 teaspoon vanilla extract
- Pinch of salt
- Whipped cream (optional, for serving)
- Ground cinnamon for dusting (optional)

Instructions:

Combine Ingredients:
- In a saucepan, combine the chopped Mexican chocolate, cocoa powder, granulated sugar, cinnamon stick, ground cinnamon (if using), vanilla extract, and a pinch of salt.

Heat Milk:
- Pour the whole milk into the saucepan over medium heat. Whisk continuously to ensure that the chocolate and other ingredients dissolve into the milk.

Bring to a Simmer:
- Continue heating the mixture, whisking regularly, until it comes to a simmer. Be careful not to let it boil over.

Simmer and Whisk:
- Once the mixture is simmering, reduce the heat to low and let it simmer for about 5-7 minutes, whisking constantly. This helps to thicken the hot chocolate.

Remove Cinnamon Stick:
- Remove the cinnamon stick from the hot chocolate.

Serve:
- Pour the Mexican Hot Chocolate into mugs. If desired, top with whipped cream and dust with ground cinnamon.

Enjoy:
- Serve immediately and enjoy the rich and spiced goodness of Mexican Hot Chocolate.

Note: Mexican chocolate often contains sugar and spices like cinnamon, which gives the hot chocolate a distinctive flavor. If using unsweetened chocolate, you may need to adjust the sugar to your liking.

Feel free to experiment with additional spices such as nutmeg or cayenne pepper for a unique twist on the traditional Mexican Hot Chocolate.

Desserts:

Tres Leches Cake Recipe

Ingredients:

For the Cake:

- 1 cup all-purpose flour
- 1 1/2 teaspoons baking powder
- 1/4 teaspoon salt
- 1/2 cup unsalted butter, softened
- 1 cup granulated sugar
- 4 large eggs
- 1 teaspoon vanilla extract

For the Three Milks Mixture:

- 1 can (14 ounces) sweetened condensed milk
- 1 can (12 ounces) evaporated milk
- 1 cup whole milk

For the Whipped Cream Topping:

- 1 1/2 cups heavy cream
- 1/2 cup powdered sugar
- 1 teaspoon vanilla extract

Instructions:

For the Cake:

Preheat the Oven:
- Preheat your oven to 350°F (175°C). Grease and flour a 9x13-inch baking dish.

Prepare Dry Ingredients:
- In a bowl, whisk together the flour, baking powder, and salt. Set aside.

Cream Butter and Sugar:
- In a large mixing bowl, cream together the softened butter and granulated sugar until light and fluffy.

Add Eggs and Vanilla:
- Add the eggs one at a time, beating well after each addition. Stir in the vanilla extract.

Incorporate Dry Ingredients:
- Gradually add the dry ingredients to the wet ingredients, mixing until just combined. Be careful not to overmix.

Bake:
- Pour the batter into the prepared baking dish and smooth the top. Bake in the preheated oven for about 25-30 minutes or until a toothpick inserted into the center comes out clean.

For the Three Milks Mixture:

Prepare the Mixture:
- In a bowl, whisk together the sweetened condensed milk, evaporated milk, and whole milk.

Poke Holes in the Cake:
- Once the cake is baked and still warm, use a fork or skewer to poke holes all over the cake.

Soak the Cake:
- Pour the three milks mixture over the warm cake, making sure to evenly distribute the liquid. Allow the cake to absorb the mixture and cool to room temperature.

For the Whipped Cream Topping:

Whip the Cream:
- In a separate bowl, whip the heavy cream, powdered sugar, and vanilla extract until stiff peaks form.

Spread Whipped Cream:
- Spread the whipped cream over the cooled cake, covering it completely.

Chill:
- Refrigerate the Tres Leches Cake for at least 2 hours or overnight to allow the flavors to meld and the cake to set.

Serve:
- Slice and serve the Tres Leches Cake cold. Enjoy the moist and delicious treat!

Note: Tres Leches Cake is often topped with fresh fruit or a sprinkle of ground cinnamon for added flavor and presentation.

Churros with Chocolate Sauce Recipe

Ingredients:

For the Churros:

- 1 cup water
- 1/2 cup unsalted butter
- 1/4 teaspoon salt
- 1 cup all-purpose flour
- 3 large eggs
- 1 teaspoon vanilla extract
- Vegetable oil, for frying
- 1/2 cup granulated sugar
- 1 teaspoon ground cinnamon

For the Chocolate Sauce:

- 1 cup heavy cream
- 8 ounces bittersweet or semisweet chocolate, finely chopped
- 2 tablespoons unsalted butter
- 1 teaspoon vanilla extract
- Pinch of salt

Instructions:

For the Churros:

Prepare Dough:
- In a saucepan, combine water, butter, and salt. Bring to a boil. Remove from heat and stir in the flour until a smooth dough forms.

Add Eggs and Vanilla:
- Let the dough cool for a few minutes, then add the eggs one at a time, beating well after each addition. Stir in the vanilla extract.

Pipe Churros:
- Heat vegetable oil in a deep fryer or large, deep skillet to 375°F (190°C). Place the churro dough into a pastry bag fitted with a star tip. Pipe 4-6 inch strips of dough into the hot oil, using scissors to cut them.

Fry until Golden Brown:
- Fry the churros until they are golden brown and crispy. Remove them with a slotted spoon and drain on paper towels.

Coat with Sugar and Cinnamon:

- In a shallow dish, combine granulated sugar and ground cinnamon. Roll the warm churros in the sugar-cinnamon mixture to coat them evenly.

For the Chocolate Sauce:

Prepare Chocolate Sauce:
- In a small saucepan, heat the heavy cream until it just begins to simmer. Remove from heat and add the finely chopped chocolate, butter, vanilla extract, and a pinch of salt. Stir until the chocolate is melted and the sauce is smooth.

Serve:
- Serve the churros warm with the chocolate sauce for dipping.

Note: Churros are best enjoyed fresh, so serve them immediately after coating in sugar and cinnamon. The chocolate sauce can be kept warm for dipping.

Feel free to adjust the sugar and cinnamon coating according to your taste preferences, and you can also add a touch of ground cinnamon to the chocolate sauce for extra flavor. Enjoy your homemade Churros with Chocolate Sauce!

Arroz con Leche Recipe

Ingredients:

- 1 cup white rice
- 4 cups whole milk
- 1 cinnamon stick
- 1/2 cup sugar (adjust to taste)
- 1 teaspoon vanilla extract
- 1/2 cup raisins (optional)
- Ground cinnamon for garnish

Instructions:

Rinse and Soak Rice:
- Rinse the rice under cold water until the water runs clear. In a bowl, soak the rice in warm water for about 15-20 minutes. Drain.

Cook Rice:
- In a medium-sized saucepan, combine the soaked and drained rice with 2 cups of water. Bring to a boil, then reduce the heat to low, cover, and simmer until the rice is cooked and most of the water is absorbed.

Add Milk and Cinnamon Stick:
- Add the whole milk and cinnamon stick to the cooked rice. Stir well and bring the mixture to a simmer over medium heat.

Simmer and Stir:
- Reduce the heat to low and simmer the rice and milk mixture, stirring frequently to prevent sticking, until it thickens. This process may take about 20-30 minutes.

Add Sugar:
- Once the rice is creamy and has absorbed most of the milk, add the sugar and continue to stir until the sugar is dissolved.

Finish Cooking:
- Continue to cook the arroz con leche until it reaches your desired consistency. Keep in mind that it will thicken further as it cools.

Add Vanilla and Raisins:
- Remove the saucepan from the heat and stir in the vanilla extract. If you're using raisins, add them at this point.

Serve:
- Remove the cinnamon stick. Serve the arroz con leche warm or chilled. It can be served in individual bowls or glasses.

Garnish:
- Garnish with a sprinkle of ground cinnamon on top of each serving.

Note: Arroz con Leche can be enjoyed warm or chilled. If you prefer a thicker consistency, you can let it cool in the refrigerator before serving.

Feel free to customize the recipe by adding a pinch of nutmeg, orange zest, or a splash of brandy for additional flavor. Enjoy this comforting and delicious dessert!

Flan Recipe

Ingredients:

For the Caramel:

- 1 cup granulated sugar
- 1/4 cup water

For the Custard:

- 4 large eggs
- 1 can (14 ounces) sweetened condensed milk
- 1 can (12 ounces) evaporated milk
- 1 tablespoon vanilla extract

Instructions:

For the Caramel:

Prepare Ramekins:
- Grease the bottom and sides of individual ramekins or a large flan mold.

Make Caramel:
- In a saucepan, combine the granulated sugar and water over medium heat. Stir until the sugar dissolves.

Caramelize Sugar:
- Allow the sugar mixture to boil without stirring. Swirl the pan occasionally to ensure even caramelization. Cook until the sugar turns into a deep amber color.

Pour Caramel into Molds:
- Quickly pour the caramel into the prepared ramekins or flan mold, swirling to coat the bottoms evenly. Work quickly, as the caramel will set fast.

For the Custard:

Preheat Oven:
- Preheat your oven to 350°F (175°C).

Prepare Custard Mixture:
- In a blender, combine the eggs, sweetened condensed milk, evaporated milk, and vanilla extract. Blend until smooth.

Strain Mixture:
- Strain the custard mixture through a fine-mesh sieve or cheesecloth into a bowl to ensure a smooth texture.

Pour Custard into Molds:
- Pour the custard mixture over the set caramel in the ramekins or flan mold.

Bake in Water Bath:
- Place the filled ramekins or flan mold in a larger baking dish. Fill the baking dish with hot water until it reaches halfway up the sides of the ramekins or mold.

Bake:
- Bake in the preheated oven for about 45-50 minutes or until the flan is set but still slightly jiggly in the center.

Cool and Refrigerate:
- Remove from the oven and allow the flan to cool to room temperature. Refrigerate for at least 4 hours or overnight.

Unmold:
- To serve, run a knife around the edges of the flan, place a serving plate over the top, and invert the flan onto the plate, allowing the caramel to drizzle over the top.

Serve:
- Slice and serve the flan chilled.

Note: Flan is traditionally served chilled, and the caramel on top forms a delicious sauce. Customize the recipe by adding a touch of cinnamon or citrus zest to the custard mixture for extra flavor. Enjoy your homemade flan!

Sopapillas Recipe

Ingredients:

- 2 cups all-purpose flour
- 1 teaspoon baking powder
- 1/2 teaspoon salt
- 2 tablespoons vegetable oil
- 3/4 cup warm water
- Vegetable oil for frying
- Honey, for drizzling
- Powdered sugar, for dusting (optional)
- Cinnamon sugar (optional)

Instructions:

Prepare the Dough:
- In a mixing bowl, whisk together the flour, baking powder, and salt.

Add Oil and Water:
- Add the vegetable oil to the dry ingredients. Gradually add the warm water, stirring continuously until a soft dough forms.

Knead the Dough:
- Turn the dough out onto a floured surface and knead it for a few minutes until it becomes smooth. Cover the dough with a damp cloth and let it rest for about 15-20 minutes.

Roll Out the Dough:
- Roll out the rested dough to about 1/8-inch thickness on a floured surface.

Cut into Squares:
- Cut the rolled-out dough into squares or rectangles, depending on your preference. A common size is about 3x3 inches.

Heat Oil for Frying:
- In a deep fryer or a deep, heavy pot, heat vegetable oil to 375°F (190°C).

Fry the Sopapillas:
- Carefully place the cut dough pieces into the hot oil, a few at a time, and fry until they puff up and turn golden brown. This usually takes about 1-2 minutes per side.

Drain and Cool:
- Use a slotted spoon to remove the fried sopapillas from the oil and drain them on paper towels.

Serve:

- Serve the sopapillas warm. Drizzle honey over the top, and if desired, dust with powdered sugar or sprinkle with cinnamon sugar.

Enjoy:
- Enjoy your homemade sopapillas as a delicious treat.

Note: Sopapillas can be served in various ways. Some people enjoy them savory with cheese or as a side dish with meals. For a sweet twist, serve them with ice cream or a side of chocolate sauce.

Feel free to get creative with the toppings and find your favorite way to enjoy sopapillas!

Mexican Wedding Cookies (Polvorones) Recipe

Ingredients:

- 1 cup unsalted butter, softened
- 1/2 cup powdered sugar, plus extra for coating
- 1 teaspoon vanilla extract
- 2 cups all-purpose flour
- 1 cup finely chopped nuts (walnuts, pecans, or almonds)
- Pinch of salt

Instructions:

Preheat Oven:
- Preheat your oven to 350°F (175°C). Line a baking sheet with parchment paper.

Cream Butter and Sugar:
- In a large mixing bowl, cream together the softened butter and powdered sugar until light and fluffy.

Add Vanilla:
- Add the vanilla extract to the butter-sugar mixture and mix until well combined.

Combine Dry Ingredients:
- In a separate bowl, whisk together the flour and a pinch of salt.

Add Nuts:
- Gradually add the flour mixture to the butter mixture, mixing until just combined. Fold in the finely chopped nuts.

Shape Cookies:
- Take small portions of the dough and roll them into balls or crescent shapes. Place the shaped cookies on the prepared baking sheet, leaving some space between them.

Bake:
- Bake in the preheated oven for about 12-15 minutes or until the edges of the cookies are lightly golden.

Cool:
- Allow the cookies to cool on the baking sheet for a few minutes before transferring them to a wire rack to cool completely.

Coat in Powdered Sugar:
- Once the cookies are completely cooled, roll them in powdered sugar to coat them generously.

Serve and Enjoy:
- Serve these Mexican Wedding Cookies on a festive platter and enjoy their buttery, nutty goodness.

Note: These cookies are delicate and crumbly, so handle them gently. You can store Mexican Wedding Cookies in an airtight container for several days, and they tend to get even better over time as the flavors meld.

Feel free to customize the recipe by using your favorite nuts or adding a touch of cinnamon for extra flavor. Enjoy these delightful treats at weddings, holidays, or any special occasion!

Coconut Tres Leches Cupcakes Recipe

Ingredients:

For the Cupcakes:

- 1 cup all-purpose flour
- 1 1/2 teaspoons baking powder
- 1/4 teaspoon salt
- 4 large eggs, separated
- 1 cup granulated sugar, divided
- 1/2 cup unsalted butter, melted
- 1/2 cup coconut milk
- 1 teaspoon vanilla extract

For the Tres Leches Soak:

- 1/2 cup coconut milk
- 1/2 cup sweetened condensed milk
- 1/2 cup evaporated milk

For the Coconut Whipped Cream:

- 1 cup heavy cream
- 1/4 cup powdered sugar
- 1/2 teaspoon coconut extract (optional)
- Shredded coconut for garnish

Instructions:

For the Cupcakes:

Preheat Oven:
- Preheat your oven to 350°F (175°C). Line a cupcake tin with cupcake liners.

Prepare Dry Ingredients:
- In a bowl, whisk together the flour, baking powder, and salt.

Beat Egg Whites:
- In a clean, dry bowl, beat the egg whites until soft peaks form. Gradually add 1/2 cup of sugar and continue beating until stiff peaks form.

Mix Wet Ingredients:

- In another bowl, whisk together the egg yolks, melted butter, coconut milk, and vanilla extract. Add the remaining 1/2 cup of sugar and mix until well combined.

Combine Batter:
- Gently fold the egg yolk mixture into the beaten egg whites. Gradually add the dry ingredients and fold until just combined.

Bake:
- Divide the batter evenly among the cupcake liners. Bake for about 18-20 minutes or until a toothpick inserted into the center comes out clean.

For the Tres Leches Soak:

Prepare Tres Leches Mixture:
- In a bowl, whisk together the coconut milk, sweetened condensed milk, and evaporated milk.

Soak Cupcakes:
- Once the cupcakes are out of the oven and still warm, use a fork or toothpick to poke several holes in each cupcake. Pour the tres leches mixture evenly over the cupcakes.

For the Coconut Whipped Cream:

Whip Cream:
- In a chilled bowl, whip the heavy cream until soft peaks form. Add powdered sugar and coconut extract (if using), and continue whipping until stiff peaks form.

Frost Cupcakes:
- Frost the cooled cupcakes with coconut whipped cream.

Garnish:
- Sprinkle shredded coconut on top of each cupcake as a garnish.

Chill:
- Refrigerate the cupcakes for at least 2 hours to allow the flavors to meld.

Serve:
- Serve these Coconut Tres Leches Cupcakes chilled and enjoy the tropical, moist goodness!

Feel free to adjust the amount of coconut extract and shredded coconut to suit your taste preferences. These cupcakes are a delightful, individual-sized version of the classic Coconut Tres Leches Cake.

Cajeta (Goat's Milk Caramel) Recipe

Ingredients:

- 4 cups goat's milk
- 1 cup granulated sugar
- 1/2 teaspoon baking soda
- 1 cinnamon stick (optional)
- 1 teaspoon vanilla extract (optional)

Instructions:

Prepare Goat's Milk:
- In a heavy-bottomed saucepan, heat the goat's milk over medium heat until it comes to a simmer. Reduce the heat to low and keep it warm.

Dissolve Baking Soda:
- In a small bowl, dissolve the baking soda in a couple of tablespoons of warm water.

Caramelize Sugar:
- In a separate, larger saucepan, heat the granulated sugar over medium heat. Allow the sugar to melt and caramelize, stirring occasionally to ensure even melting.

Add Baking Soda:
- Once the sugar has turned into a golden-brown caramel, carefully add the dissolved baking soda to the saucepan. Be cautious, as the mixture may bubble up.

Slowly Add Goat's Milk:
- Gradually and carefully add the warm goat's milk to the caramelized sugar, stirring constantly to avoid lumps. Add the cinnamon stick if using.

Simmer:
- Bring the mixture to a simmer over low heat. Stir frequently to prevent sticking and burning.

Cook Until Thickened:
- Allow the mixture to simmer and reduce, stirring occasionally, until it reaches a thick, caramel-like consistency. This may take 1 to 1.5 hours.

Add Vanilla (Optional):
- If desired, stir in vanilla extract during the last few minutes of cooking for added flavor.

Remove Cinnamon Stick:
- If you used a cinnamon stick, remove it from the Cajeta.

Cool and Store:
- Let the Cajeta cool to room temperature. Transfer it to sterilized jars or containers for storage.

Serve:
- Use Cajeta as a topping for desserts, pancakes, ice cream, or as a filling for pastries. Enjoy the rich and luscious flavor of homemade goat's milk caramel!

Note: Cajeta will thicken further as it cools. Store it in the refrigerator for longer shelf life. Cajeta is a versatile sauce and can be used in various desserts and sweet treats.

Pineapple Empanadas Recipe

Ingredients:

For the Filling:

- 2 cups fresh pineapple, finely chopped
- 1/2 cup granulated sugar
- 1 tablespoon cornstarch
- 1/2 teaspoon ground cinnamon
- 1/4 teaspoon salt
- 1 tablespoon lemon juice

For the Empanada Dough:

- 2 cups all-purpose flour
- 1/4 cup granulated sugar
- 1/2 teaspoon salt
- 3/4 cup unsalted butter, cold and cut into small pieces
- 1/4 cup cold water
- 1 teaspoon white vinegar
- 1 large egg (for egg wash)

For Dusting:

- Powdered sugar (optional)

Instructions:

For the Filling:

Prepare Pineapple:
- In a bowl, combine the finely chopped fresh pineapple, granulated sugar, cornstarch, ground cinnamon, salt, and lemon juice. Mix well and set aside to let the flavors meld.

For the Empanada Dough:

Prepare Dough:

- In a large bowl, whisk together the flour, sugar, and salt. Add the cold, chopped butter, and use your fingers or a pastry cutter to incorporate the butter into the flour until the mixture resembles coarse crumbs.

Add Water and Vinegar:
- In a small bowl, mix together the cold water and white vinegar. Gradually add the water mixture to the flour mixture, stirring with a fork until the dough starts to come together.

Form Dough:
- Turn the dough out onto a floured surface and knead it a few times until it comes together. Shape it into a disk, wrap it in plastic wrap, and refrigerate for at least 30 minutes.

Preheat Oven:
- Preheat your oven to 375°F (190°C). Line a baking sheet with parchment paper.

Roll Out Dough:
- On a floured surface, roll out the chilled dough to about 1/8 inch thickness. Use a round cutter to cut out circles for the empanadas.

Fill and Seal Empanadas:
- Place a spoonful of the pineapple filling in the center of each dough circle. Fold the dough over the filling to create a half-moon shape. Seal the edges with a fork or by crimping with your fingers.

Brush with Egg Wash:
- Beat the egg and brush it over the tops of the empanadas for a golden finish.

Bake:
- Place the filled empanadas on the prepared baking sheet and bake for about 15-18 minutes or until they are golden brown.

Cool and Dust (Optional):
- Allow the Pineapple Empanadas to cool slightly before serving. Optionally, dust with powdered sugar for a sweet touch.

Serve and Enjoy:
- Serve these delicious Pineapple Empanadas as a delightful dessert or snack.

These Pineapple Empanadas are a perfect treat for those who love the combination of sweet and tart flavors. Customize the recipe by adding a sprinkle of cinnamon sugar on top or serving with a scoop of vanilla ice cream.

Mexican Chocolate Mousse Recipe

Ingredients:

- 8 ounces (about 225g) bittersweet chocolate, finely chopped
- 1/4 cup unsweetened cocoa powder
- 1/2 teaspoon ground cinnamon
- 1/4 teaspoon chili powder (adjust to taste)
- Pinch of cayenne pepper
- 1/4 cup strong brewed coffee, cooled
- 4 large eggs, separated
- 1/2 cup granulated sugar
- 1 teaspoon vanilla extract
- 1 cup heavy cream
- Whipped cream and chocolate shavings for garnish (optional)

Instructions:

Prepare Chocolate Mixture:

- In a heatproof bowl, combine the finely chopped bittersweet chocolate, cocoa powder, ground cinnamon, chili powder, and cayenne pepper.

Add Coffee:

- Pour the cooled brewed coffee over the chocolate mixture. Allow it to sit for a minute to soften the chocolate.

Melt Chocolate:

- Gently melt the chocolate by placing the bowl over a pot of simmering water (double boiler). Stir until smooth and well combined. Remove from heat and let it cool slightly.

Whip Egg Yolks:

- In a separate bowl, whisk the egg yolks with half of the granulated sugar until pale and slightly thickened.

Temper Chocolate:
- Gradually whisk the melted chocolate mixture into the egg yolk mixture to temper the eggs.

Add Vanilla:
- Stir in the vanilla extract into the chocolate and egg yolk mixture.

Whip Egg Whites:
- In another clean, dry bowl, whip the egg whites until soft peaks form. Gradually add the remaining sugar and continue whipping until glossy and stiff peaks form.

Fold in Egg Whites:
- Gently fold the whipped egg whites into the chocolate mixture until well combined. Be gentle to maintain the mousse's light and airy texture.

Whip Cream:
- In a separate bowl, whip the heavy cream until stiff peaks form.

Fold in Whipped Cream:
- Gently fold the whipped cream into the chocolate mixture until smooth and well incorporated.

Chill:
- Divide the mousse into serving glasses or bowls. Chill in the refrigerator for at least 4 hours or until set.

Garnish (Optional):
- Before serving, garnish the Mexican Chocolate Mousse with whipped cream and chocolate shavings, if desired.

Serve and Enjoy:
- Serve this decadent Mexican Chocolate Mousse chilled and savor the rich and spicy chocolate flavors.

Feel free to adjust the level of chili powder and cayenne pepper according to your taste preferences. This dessert is a delightful way to end a Mexican-themed meal or to enjoy a special treat.

Beverages:

Horchata

Ingredients:

- 1 cup long-grain white rice
- 5 cups water
- 1 cinnamon stick
- 1/2 cup granulated sugar (adjust to taste)
- 1 teaspoon vanilla extract (optional)
- Ground cinnamon for garnish

Instructions:

Rinse the Rice:
- Rinse the rice under cold water to remove excess starch.

Soak the Rice:
- In a blender, combine the rinsed rice and 2 cups of water. Blend until the rice is broken down but not completely smooth. It should have a gritty texture.
- Transfer the rice mixture to a bowl and add the cinnamon stick. Add the remaining 3 cups of water, cover the bowl, and let it soak at room temperature for at least 3 hours or preferably overnight.

Blend and Strain:
- After soaking, blend the rice mixture again until it forms a smoother liquid.
- Strain the mixture through a fine-mesh sieve or cheesecloth into a pitcher, separating the liquid from the rice solids. You may need to do this in batches.

Sweeten the Horchata:
- Add sugar to the strained liquid and stir until the sugar is fully dissolved. You can adjust the amount of sugar to your taste.

Add Vanilla Extract (Optional):
- If you like, add vanilla extract for extra flavor. Stir to combine.

Chill:
- Refrigerate the horchata for at least 2 hours or until it's thoroughly chilled.

Serve:

- Before serving, stir the horchata well as it may settle. Pour it over ice and sprinkle ground cinnamon on top.

Enjoy:
- Enjoy your homemade horchata as a refreshing beverage.

Horchata is a versatile drink, and variations exist in different regions. Some people like to add a touch of ground cinnamon directly to the mixture or serve it with a dusting of ground cinnamon on top. Experiment with the sweetness and flavors to suit your preferences.

Agua Fresca (e.g., Jamaica, Tamarindo)

Jamaica (Hibiscus) Agua Fresca:

Ingredients:

- 1 cup dried hibiscus flowers (Jamaica)
- 4 cups water
- 1/2 to 3/4 cup granulated sugar (adjust to taste)
- Ice cubes
- Fresh mint leaves for garnish (optional)
- Lime wedges for serving (optional)

Instructions:

Prepare Hibiscus Infusion:
- In a pot, bring 4 cups of water to a boil.
- Add the dried hibiscus flowers to the boiling water, turn off the heat, and let it steep for about 15-20 minutes.

Strain and Sweeten:
- Strain the hibiscus infusion to remove the flowers, pressing them to extract as much flavor as possible.
- Sweeten the hibiscus water with sugar, starting with 1/2 cup and adjusting to your desired sweetness. Stir until the sugar is dissolved.

Chill:
- Allow the Jamaica Agua Fresca to cool, then refrigerate until well chilled.

Serve:
- Serve over ice, garnish with fresh mint leaves, and optionally, serve with lime wedges.

Tamarindo (Tamarind) Agua Fresca:

Ingredients:

- 1 cup tamarind pulp (from about 1/2 pound tamarind pods)
- 4 cups water
- 1/2 to 3/4 cup granulated sugar (adjust to taste)
- Ice cubes
- Lime wedges for serving (optional)

Instructions:

Extract Tamarind Pulp:
- Remove the tamarind pulp from the tamarind pods. Place the pulp in a bowl and add 2 cups of warm water. Let it sit for about 15 minutes, mashing the pulp with your hands to extract flavor.

Strain and Sweeten:
- Strain the tamarind mixture into a pitcher, pressing the pulp to extract all the liquid.
- Add an additional 2 cups of water to the strained tamarind liquid.
- Sweeten with sugar, starting with 1/2 cup and adjusting to your desired sweetness. Stir until the sugar is dissolved.

Chill:
- Allow the Tamarindo Agua Fresca to cool, then refrigerate until well chilled.

Serve:
- Serve over ice and optionally, serve with lime wedges.

Agua Fresca is a delightful and hydrating beverage, perfect for warm days. Feel free to adjust the sweetness and customize the flavors to your liking. Enjoy!

Margarita:

Ingredients:

- 2 oz (60 ml) tequila
- 1 oz (30 ml) triple sec or orange liqueur
- 1 oz (30 ml) freshly squeezed lime juice
- 1/2 oz (15 ml) simple syrup (adjust to taste)
- Ice
- Salt for rimming the glass (optional)
- Lime wedge for garnish

Instructions:

    Rim the Glass (Optional):
- If you like, moisten the rim of a glass with a lime wedge and dip it into salt to coat the rim.

    Prepare the Cocktail:
- In a cocktail shaker, combine tequila, triple sec, freshly squeezed lime juice, and simple syrup.

    Add Ice and Shake:
- Fill the shaker with ice and shake the ingredients well to chill the mixture.

    Strain and Serve:
- Strain the cocktail into the prepared glass over ice.

    Garnish:
- Garnish with a lime wedge.

    Optional Variation - Frozen Margarita:
- To make a frozen Margarita, blend the ingredients with ice until smooth. Adjust the ice quantity to achieve your desired consistency.

Variations:

- Flavored Margaritas: Experiment with different fruit flavors by adding a splash of fruit juice (such as orange, mango, or pineapple) or using flavored liqueurs.
- Spicy Margarita: Add a slice of jalapeño or a dash of hot sauce for a spicy kick.
- Margarita on the Rocks: Serve the Margarita over ice for a classic on-the-rocks version.
- Margarita Pitcher: Multiply the ingredients to make a pitcher for a group.

Remember to adjust the sweetness and acidity to suit your taste preferences. Cheers and enjoy responsibly!

Michelada:

Ingredients:

- 1 Mexican lager beer (e.g., Corona, Modelo)
- 1 oz (30 ml) freshly squeezed lime juice
- 1 dash Worcestershire sauce
- 1 dash hot sauce (e.g., Tabasco)
- Tajín or salt, for rimming the glass
- Ice
- Optional: Clamato juice for added flavor

Instructions:

Rim the Glass:
- If you'd like, moisten the rim of a chilled, tall glass with a lime wedge, and dip it into Tajín or salt to coat the rim.

Prepare the Cocktail:
- Squeeze the juice from a lime and add it to the glass.
- Add a dash of Worcestershire sauce and a dash of hot sauce to the glass.

Add Ice:
- Fill the glass with ice.

Pour Beer:
- Pour the Mexican lager beer into the glass. Pour it slowly to control the foam.

Optional: Add Clamato Juice:
- Some variations of Michelada include Clamato juice for a savory and slightly briny flavor. You can add a splash if desired.

Stir Gently:
- Use a stirring stick or spoon to gently mix the ingredients in the glass.

Garnish:
- Garnish the Michelada with a lime wedge on the rim.

Serve:
- Serve and enjoy your refreshing Michelada!

Variations:

- Chamoy Michelada: Add chamoy sauce for a sweet and tangy twist.
- Cucumber Michelada: Include cucumber slices or cucumber juice for a cool and crisp flavor.

- Spicy Michelada: Experiment with different hot sauces or add slices of fresh jalapeño for an extra kick.

Micheladas are highly customizable, so feel free to adjust the ingredients and proportions to suit your taste preferences. Cheers!

Mexican Hot Chocolate:

Ingredients:

- 2 cups whole milk
- 2 ounces (about 60 grams) Mexican chocolate, coarsely chopped (such as Abuelita or Ibarra)
- 1 to 2 tablespoons granulated sugar (adjust to taste)
- 1/2 teaspoon ground cinnamon
- 1/4 teaspoon vanilla extract (optional)
- Pinch of cayenne pepper (optional, for a hint of spice)
- Whipped cream, for topping (optional)
- Ground cinnamon, for garnish

Instructions:

Heat Milk:
- In a saucepan over medium heat, warm the milk until it's just about to simmer. Be careful not to boil it.

Add Chocolate:
- Add the chopped Mexican chocolate to the warm milk.

Whisk and Melt:
- Whisk the chocolate into the milk until it's completely melted and well combined.

Add Sugar and Spices:
- Stir in the granulated sugar, ground cinnamon, vanilla extract (if using), and a pinch of cayenne pepper if you want a bit of spice. Adjust the sugar to your desired sweetness.

Whisk Until Frothy:
- Continue to whisk the mixture over medium heat until it becomes frothy. This can take a few minutes.

Remove from Heat:
- Once the hot chocolate is well combined and frothy, remove it from the heat.

Serve:
- Pour the Mexican Hot Chocolate into mugs.

Top and Garnish:
- Optionally, top each mug with whipped cream and sprinkle a little ground cinnamon for garnish.

Enjoy:

- Serve immediately and enjoy your comforting and spiced Mexican Hot Chocolate!

Variation:

- Abuelita or Ibarra Tablets: If you're using Mexican chocolate tablets like Abuelita or Ibarra, you can melt the tablet directly into the warm milk, stirring until it's completely dissolved.

Mexican Hot Chocolate has a unique blend of spices and is a delicious treat, especially during colder seasons. Adjust the spice and sweetness levels to your liking, and savor the rich flavors of this traditional beverage.

Atole:

Ingredients:

- 1/2 cup masa harina (corn flour)
- 4 cups water or milk (or a combination of both)
- 1 cinnamon stick
- 1/2 cup piloncillo (Mexican unrefined cane sugar) or brown sugar (adjust to taste)
- 1 teaspoon vanilla extract
- Ground cinnamon for garnish (optional)

Instructions:

Prepare Masa Paste:
- In a small bowl, mix the masa harina with a small amount of water to create a smooth paste.

Combine Masa Paste with Water or Milk:
- In a saucepan, combine the masa paste with 4 cups of water or milk (or a combination of both). Whisk well to avoid lumps.

Add Cinnamon Stick:
- Add the cinnamon stick to the mixture.

Heat and Simmer:
- Place the saucepan over medium heat and bring the mixture to a simmer. Stir frequently to prevent sticking.

Sweeten with Piloncillo or Brown Sugar:
- Once the mixture is simmering, add the piloncillo or brown sugar. Adjust the sweetness to your liking. Continue stirring until the sugar is completely dissolved.

Flavor with Vanilla:
- Stir in the vanilla extract.

Continue Cooking:
- Allow the Atole to simmer for about 10-15 minutes, or until it thickens to your desired consistency. Keep stirring to prevent lumps.

Remove Cinnamon Stick:
- Remove the cinnamon stick from the Atole.

Serve:
- Pour the Atole into mugs or cups.

Garnish (Optional):
- Garnish with a sprinkle of ground cinnamon on top if desired.

Enjoy:
- Serve the Atole hot and enjoy this comforting and traditional Mexican beverage!

Flavor Variations:

- Chocolate Atole (Atole de Chocolate): Add cocoa powder or grated Mexican chocolate to the mixture for a delicious chocolate-flavored Atole.
- Vanilla Atole (Atole de Vainilla): Enhance the vanilla flavor by adding an extra splash of vanilla extract.

Atole is often enjoyed as a breakfast or dessert beverage and is perfect for warming up on chilly days. Feel free to experiment with flavors and sweeteners to suit your taste preferences.

Champurrado:

Ingredients:

- 1/2 cup masa harina (corn flour)
- 4 cups water
- 1 cinnamon stick
- 1 Mexican chocolate tablet (such as Abuelita or Ibarra), chopped
- 1/2 cup piloncillo (Mexican unrefined cane sugar) or brown sugar (adjust to taste)
- 1 teaspoon vanilla extract
- Ground cinnamon for garnish (optional)

Instructions:

Prepare Masa Paste:
- In a small bowl, mix the masa harina with a small amount of water to create a smooth paste.

Combine Masa Paste with Water:
- In a saucepan, combine the masa paste with 4 cups of water. Whisk well to avoid lumps.

Add Cinnamon Stick:
- Add the cinnamon stick to the mixture.

Heat and Simmer:
- Place the saucepan over medium heat and bring the mixture to a simmer. Stir frequently to prevent sticking.

Add Chocolate:
- Once the mixture is simmering, add the chopped Mexican chocolate. Continue stirring until the chocolate is completely melted.

Sweeten with Piloncillo or Brown Sugar:
- Add the piloncillo or brown sugar to the Champurrado. Adjust the sweetness to your liking. Continue stirring until the sugar is dissolved.

Flavor with Vanilla:
- Stir in the vanilla extract.

Continue Cooking:
- Allow the Champurrado to simmer for about 10-15 minutes, or until it thickens to your desired consistency. Keep stirring to prevent lumps.

Remove Cinnamon Stick:
- Remove the cinnamon stick from the Champurrado.

Serve:

- Pour the Champurrado into mugs or cups.

Garnish (Optional):
- Garnish with a sprinkle of ground cinnamon on top if desired.

Enjoy:
- Serve the Champurrado hot and savor the rich and comforting flavors!

Champurrado is a delightful and festive beverage, especially enjoyed during the holiday season. Adjust the sweetness and thickness according to your preferences, and enjoy this traditional Mexican treat.

Café de Olla:

Ingredients:

- 4 cups water
- 1/2 cup coarsely ground coffee (Mexican coffee beans, if available)
- 1 to 2 cinnamon sticks
- 4-6 whole cloves
- 1 piloncillo cone (Mexican unrefined cane sugar) or 1/2 cup brown sugar (adjust to taste)
- Optional: Orange peel or a piece of star anise for extra flavor

Instructions:

Prepare Water and Sugar:
- In a saucepan, combine the water and piloncillo (or brown sugar). If using piloncillo, break it into smaller pieces for easier dissolving.

Add Spices:
- Add the coarsely ground coffee, cinnamon sticks, whole cloves, and any optional spices like orange peel or star anise.

Bring to a Boil:
- Place the saucepan over medium-high heat and bring the mixture to a boil.

Simmer:
- Once it boils, reduce the heat to low and let it simmer for about 5-10 minutes to allow the flavors to infuse.

Remove from Heat:
- After simmering, remove the saucepan from the heat.

Strain:
- Using a fine-mesh sieve or coffee filter, strain the coffee into a coffee pot or serving pitcher. This step helps remove the coffee grounds and spices.

Serve:
- Pour the Café de Olla into mugs or cups.

Enjoy:
- Savor the rich and spiced flavors of Mexican Café de Olla!

Variation:

- Mexican Mocha: To make a Mexican Mocha, add a tablespoon of cocoa powder to the coffee mixture before straining. You can also top it with whipped cream for an extra indulgence.

Mexican coffee is often enjoyed with sweet pastries or traditional Mexican breakfast foods. Adjust the sweetness and spice levels to suit your taste preferences and experience the warm and comforting flavors of this traditional beverage.

Jarritos Paloma:

Ingredients:

- 2 oz tequila
- 1 oz fresh lime juice
- 4 oz grapefruit-flavored Jarritos soda
- Ice
- Grapefruit slice for garnish
- Salt for rimming the glass (optional)

Instructions:

> Prepare Glass (Optional):
> - If you like, rim the glass with salt by moistening the rim with a lime wedge and dipping it in salt.
>
> Build the Cocktail:
> - Fill the glass with ice.
>
> Add Tequila and Lime Juice:
> - Pour the tequila and fresh lime juice over the ice.
>
> Top with Jarritos:
> - Top the cocktail with grapefruit-flavored Jarritos soda.
>
> Stir Gently:
> - Give the mixture a gentle stir to combine the ingredients.
>
> Garnish:
> - Garnish with a slice of grapefruit on the rim.
>
> Enjoy:
> - Enjoy the refreshing Jarritos Paloma!

Jarritos Margarita:

Ingredients:

- 2 oz tequila
- 1 oz triple sec or orange liqueur
- 1 oz fresh lime juice
- 4 oz lime-flavored Jarritos soda
- Ice
- Lime wedge for garnish
- Salt for rimming the glass (optional)

Instructions:

Prepare Glass (Optional):
- If desired, rim the glass with salt by moistening the rim with a lime wedge and dipping it in salt.

Build the Cocktail:
- Fill the glass with ice.

Add Tequila, Triple Sec, and Lime Juice:
- Pour the tequila, triple sec or orange liqueur, and fresh lime juice over the ice.

Top with Jarritos:
- Top the cocktail with lime-flavored Jarritos soda.

Stir Gently:
- Give the mixture a gentle stir to combine the ingredients.

Garnish:
- Garnish with a lime wedge on the rim.

Enjoy:
- Savor the delightful Jarritos Margarita!

Feel free to adjust the ingredient quantities to suit your taste preferences. These cocktails offer a fun and colorful twist by incorporating the vibrant flavors of Jarritos sodas. Cheers!

www.ingramcontent.com/pod-product-compliance
Lightning Source LLC
LaVergne TN
LVHW081550060526
838201LV00054B/1834